Physicians for Human Rights

The Fortune Society

UNJUST AND COUNTERPRODUCTIVE

New York's Rockefeller Drug Laws

CONTENTS

Acknowledgments

This report was written by Rachel Porter, Graduate Center, City University of New York; with contributions by Ingrid Tamm, MA, Research Associate, Physicians for Human Rights (PHR); Jennifer Lin, MHS, Senior Director of Research and Evaluation, The Fortune Society (Fortune); Douglas Ford, JD, Former Senior Research Associate, PHR; and Vincent Iacopino, MD, PhD, Director of Research, PHR. The report was edited by Ms. Tamm, JoAnne Page, JD, Executive Director, Fortune; Dr. Iacopino and Chen Reis, JD, MPH, Senior Research Associate at PHR. Research was conducted by Steven Caughman, Fortune co-interviewer; Mr. Ford; Derrick Harrington, Fortune co-interviewer; David C. Leven, JD, former Executive Director, Prisoners' Legal Services of New York; Paul Rocklin, JD, Program Associate, PHR; Ms. Porter; Stanley Richards, Deputy Executive Director, Fortune; and Kenneth White, Fortune co-interviewer.

The report was reviewed by Barbara Ayotte, Director of Communications, PHR; Robert L. Cohen, MD; Ernest Drucker, PhD, Montefiore Medical Center and the Albert Einstein College of Medicine; Gina Cummings, Director of Constituency Outreach, PHR; Leonard S. Rubenstein, JD, Executive Director, PHR; Susannah Sirkin, MEd, Deputy Director, PHR. Thanks also to Jim Cho of Families Against Mandatory Minimums (FAMM) for providing the authors with FAMM case files to PHR intern Lisa Kehe for her research assistance and Erica Perel for legal analysis.

Physicians for Human Rights and The Fortune Society thank all those who participated in the study and shared their stories. We are deeply grateful to the JEHT Foundation and to the Open Society Institute for their financial support of this study.

Physicians for Human Rights

Physicians for Human Rights (PHR) promotes health by protecting human rights. PHR believes that respect for human rights is essential for the health and well-being of all people.

Since 1986, PHR members have worked to stop torture, disappearances, and political killings by governments and opposition groups and to investigate and expose violations, including: deaths, injuries, and trauma inflicted on civilians during conflicts; suffering and deprivation, including denial of access to health care, caused by ethnic and racial discrimination; mental and physical anguish inflicted on women by abuse; exploitation of children in labor practices; loss of life or limb from landmines and other indiscriminate weapons; harsh methods of incarceration in prisons and detention centers; and poor health stemming form vast inequalities in societies. As one of the original steering committee members of the International Campaign to Ban Landmines, PHR shared the 1997 Nobel Peace Prize.

Physicians for Human Rights
100 Boylston Street, Suite 702
Boston, MA 02116
Tel. 617 695-0041
Fax. 617 695-0307
Email: phrusa@phrusa.org
www.phrusa.org

The Fortune Society

The Fortune Society exists to help prisoners, ex-prisoners, and those facing jail or prison time. The Fortune Society works to improve prison conditions and protect the rights of prisoners. Staffed primarily by ex-prisoners, we are committed to providing the foundation from which new lives can be launched.

The Fortune Society seeks to reverse current punitive criminal justice policy, and to address the root causes of crime through outreach and advocacy.

Fortune is committed to having its services and advocacy shaped by the prison and transition experiences of ex-prisoners. The Fortune Society recognizes the importance of prevention by developing services that reflect the needs of our clients and their families. Fortune acts to reverse the current plague of prison construction and mass incarceration by changing minds and building lives.

The Fortune Society
53 West 23rd Street, 8th Floor
New York, NY 10010
Tel. 212 691-7554
Fax. 212 255-4948
www.fortunesociety.org

I. EXECUTIVE SUMMARY

Purpose of the Study

New York's Rockefeller drug laws were created to deter drug crimes by establishing some of the toughest mandatory minimum prison sentences in the nation. But as the findings of this study illustrate, the compulsory sentencing under Rockefeller drug laws has failed to reduce recidivism. Instead, the laws have resulted in individuals, the majority of whom are minorities struggling with drug use and poverty, trapped in a cycle of prison time and unsuccessful reintegration into society. Lengthy mandatory sentences and, more commonly, the cumulative effect of multiple incarcerations for low-level drug crimes, have a devastating effect on individuals, their families and their communities and are often disproportionate punishments to the crimes committed.

The State of New York maintains tougher mandatory minimum sentences for some repeat felony drug offenders than for offenders convicted of rape or attempted murder. As a consequence, New York's prisons are filled with people convicted of drug felonies. In 2003, nearly 38 percent of people sent to state prison went for drug offenses.[1]

Most political and media attention has focused on long sentences handed down to the most severe category of offenders. But the majority of people incarcerated for drug offenses in New York state prisons are convicted of lower level felony offenses, as were the people interviewed for this study. Little survey work has been done to paint a full picture of the persons who are incarcerated by these laws, including their lives before prison, their experiences during and after incarceration, and the effects of imprisonment on their families and communities. Physicians for Human Rights and The Fortune Society conducted qualitative interviews with fifty men and women who served at least one year in a New York state prison for a nonviolent drug offense.

---

[1] For trends of prison commitments between 1980 and 2003, see The Correctional Association of New York, *Trends in New York State Prison Commitments*, Correctional Association, February, 2004.

Prison experiences do not provide individuals with the skills, treatment or support networks that they need to break the cycle and often even reinforce drug use and criminal activity. Seventy percent of the people interviewed for this report had attempted re-entry into society on parole before their most recent release and had then been either returned to prison for a new crime or for a parole violation.

Everyone interviewed for this study was a drug user and nearly everyone struggled with addiction. Drug use and addiction represent a formidable public health problem in addition to other social, economic and political challenges. Yet drug addiction is treated first as a law enforcement problem in New York and in the United States as a whole. All too often, the public health and poverty implications of the drug trade are ignored or treated with inadequate resources.

Physicians for Human Rights and The Fortune Society recommend that the State of New York reform the Rockefeller drug laws by granting judges discretion to depart from statutory sentencing ranges, especially in cases of nonviolent drug felony offenses where people are not involved as major players in drug crimes. The groups also recommend that the State of New York work to expand, strengthen and improve alternatives for incarceration, especially for people who need drug treatment. Ending the cycle involves judicial discretion not only for departing from mandatory sentence ranges but also the discretion to divert offenders to treatment programs rather than prison.

Background

Enacted in 1973 under New York's Governor Nelson Rockefeller, the Rockefeller drug laws require disproportionately lengthy prison terms for the sale or possession of relatively small amounts of drugs. Under these sentencing mandates, judges have extremely limited discretion and must use mandatory minimum sentences for drug felonies according to the type and weight of drugs found in connection with the alleged offense, regardless of whether the judge agrees that the sentence is appropriate. For example, a judge must impose a prison term of no less than fifteen years to life for anyone convicted of selling two ounces or possessing four ounces of a controlled substance such as cocaine.

In New York, as in the rest of the country, the vast majority of drug convictions are the result of plea bargains worked out between prosecutors and defendants rather than as a result of trials. In exchange for forgoing a trial, the defendant pleads guilty and receives a sentence that is less than what the defendant would receive if convicted at trial. Indeed, 96 percent of those interviewed by PHR/Fortune waived their right to a jury trial and were sentenced according to plea negotiations. Plea bargains are coercive in the context of harsh mandatory minimum sentences because the stakes are so high if the individual is convicted at trial. Furthermore, because New York mandates longer prison sentences for felonies committed by people with a prior felony record, a guilty plea to avoid a lengthy sentence the first time around may result in tougher sentences should the person re-enter the criminal justice system.

The media frequently reports on people convicted of A1 felony offenses, the most serious in the state's penal code, for relatively small amounts of drugs that are sent to state prison for fifteen years to life. These long sentences have generated outrage and some modest reforms at the A1 level, but such cases do not represent the full extent of the problem. Instead, the majority of people incarcerated for drug offenses in New York state prisons are convicted for lower felony offenses for sometimes minute amounts of drugs (Class B, C, D, or E felonies). As a result of multiple, nonviolent small-scale drug offenses and plea bargaining, respondents described lives of repeated incarcerations in state prisons. With an average of 41 years of age, respondents had spent an average of almost half (46 percent) of their adult lives incarcerated. Drug-related prison time accounted for 78 percent of their time served, or more than a third (35 percent) of their adult lives. This does not take into account the time they spent under parole supervision.

The Rockefeller drug laws mainly affect the poor and minorities. According to correctional statistics, 93 percent of the people locked up in New York for drug offenses are African American or Latino.[2] The PHR/Fortune study mirrored these state statistics, with 60 percent of the sample African-American and 28 percent Latino. It is important to note that the people easiest to target in policing efforts are those who tend to commit street-level drug offenses – predominantly the poor and minorities. Nationally, the numbers of white drug users exceeds that of African-American users.

The Rockefeller drug laws not only affect individuals, they also affect families, as well as the largely poor, minority communities from which the vast majority of people tried under these laws are drawn. All respondents spoke about the misery of incarceration. Whether the difficulty of separation from family, the dangerous conditions to which they were exposed, the abuse they witnessed or the emotional toughening they underwent, respondents described lives of often petty crimes and addiction interrupted — but not ameliorated or resolved — by incarceration. Families lose sons, brothers, husbands and fathers; communities lose potential leadership and economic power, schools lose parental involvement. In addition, the impact of imprisonment continues after release. Restrictions on voting

---

[2] PHR obtained NYS Department of Correctional Services statistics for persons under custody for drug offenses as of December 31, 2003: of 17,081 total, 15,809 (92.5 percent) were African-American or Hispanic and 1,025 were white (6 percent).

Cycling In and Out: LY's Story

LY typifies the experiences of those who cycle in and out of prison for drug offenses, illustrating the complexities of the problem and how incarcerations often feed the cycle of addiction and recidivism.

LY, a 47-year-old African-American man, spent just over sixteen years in prison between 1977 and 2002. LY was incarcerated five separate times: four for drug sales (four years on the first sentence; three years each on the subsequent three sentences) and also one three-year sentence for burglary. At the time of the interview he was on parole having been referred to The Fortune Society as a condition of his release.

Growing up, LY had four siblings and says it was a "struggle" for his mother, who was receiving public assistance. He did not know his father. When his mother got a job as a nurse's aide, she "got off PA [public assistance]" but put in long hours. He remembers seeing her for four hours a day at most.

He started dealing drugs at age 16 "because I needed clothes to go to school and my mother couldn't afford to provide them." He dropped out of high school in the 11th grade, at age 17, "because I was hustling." "My brothers and sisters were doing the same thing I was doing — hustling." Their mother "wasn't happy about us hustling. She didn't accept the gifts we gave her."

LY had started using cocaine and marijuana at 16, "as a casual thing. Just Friday nights and Saturday nights, like people enjoy liquor. It progressed, though." He was making money from selling heroin and "out of curiosity one day, I used the heroin. I didn't like it. Then I tried it again and I did like it. That started something different. At first, I was out to make a profit to take care of the family, the kids [his girlfriend at the time had two children]. Now I was trying to support my habit, too. I was out there more than I would otherwise." Of his serious girlfriend at the time, he said, "We started coming apart when I was addicted. Addicts don't care about anything — love, relationships, anything. She didn't know at first what to say, though. She wasn't able to buy anything for [her two] kids. The habit made me less interested in taking care of her. But I did it anyway. We fell out of love but stayed together. When I got arrested, I guess that was her walking papers."

At 21, after failing a residential treatment program, LY received a sentence for a Class C felony sale, for which he served four years. He was first detained in the Rikers Island jail before he was sentenced to state prison. Of Rikers, he said, "It was okay. I was familiar with it. Then I went upstate. I was frightened but I couldn't show it. It's not the place to show it. If they see you're afraid, they categorize you as a chump, make you a clown, make fun of you and take their misery out on you. They take your stuff. Weakness shows in how you carry yourself, how you talk, how you treat people. Strength is going along with the program, not stressing, not crying. Go along with the program. It's a masquerade. You hide your anger." He went through a seven-day detoxification program at Rikers with methadone, but said that there were no drug treatment programs available to him during his first state prison incarceration.

LY was rearrested for dealing heroin sixty days after his release. He took the case against him to trial, spending a year in jail through the duration of the proceedings. In the end, he was acquitted of the sale charges and convicted on possession charges. Three more periods of incarceration followed. For his last conviction, LY was charged with attempted sale to an undercover officer and pled guilty, "I could have beat this but I couldn't because of my past criminal history. The judge said, 'if you go to trial they're going to send you up for a long time because of your past history.'" LY was then sent to "Rikers medical because of a circulation problem in my leg and liver problem from drug use." He spent 18 months at Rikers and then 18 months at Green Haven Correctional Facility, a maximum security prison, first in the hospital, then in population at Green Haven.

There he did not participate in any programs. "I was still not able to walk. I was in a wheelchair. The CO's [correctional officers] treated me okay 'til I was out of the wheelchair. Then they started treating me badly." His family did not want him to call them; they were tired of him being in prison.

Of his previous parole experiences, he says, "The parole board was not concerned with my addiction, just my crime record. I felt bad, used, stupid. I'm why these people [corrections staff] have a job." LY says that finally, in June 2002, a member of the parole board asked "'what's the problem?' I explained to her that it was my drug problem. She said, 'I'm going to parole you to a residential program because that's what you need.'" He was paroled to the Osborne Association and then referred to The Fortune Society.

Of prison and his struggle with drug addiction and sales, he says, "In five bids [prison incarcerations], I watched the CO's sons become COs. Meanwhile, I'm the one that pays rent for them because I can't get my s—— together."

LY's future plans include "staying out of jail" and taking classes at The Fortune Society, where he was residing at the time of the interview. HIV positive since 1994, he wants to "educate people about the virus."

rights, access to public housing, child custody rights, and other denials of benefits further punish people upon release from prison. These restrictions hinder both reintegration of the ex-prisoner into society and the community's ability to restore relations with them.

Alternatives to incarceration exist, such as those programs provided through drug courts and direct service providers. These alternatives aim to increase individual responsibility and the humanity of the penal system while decreasing re-offending and reducing the costs associated with incarceration. Many of these alternatives tailor their services to the individual needs of their clients, and therefore address a range of social needs beyond rehabilitation including education, healthcare, parenting and job development. Policy makers, treatment providers and criminal justice experts have lauded several of the programs described in this report, yet all are underutilized because of funding limitations and structural impediments established by mandatory sentencing laws.

The Rockefeller drug laws have many critics – including members of the judiciary, the New York State Legislature, and advocacy organizations. Such critics have long argued that these laws are ineffective, racially biased, and target the lowest-level offenders who are often poor, from minority groups, and/or suffering from drug addiction and who would be more effectively rehabilitated by alternatives to incarceration. This study joins the call to reform by showcasing, in their own words, the experiences of people cycling in and out of New York's state prisons for nonviolent drug crimes.

In sum, the Rockefeller drug laws have led to punishments that do not appear to advance the common goal of reducing recidivism but instead have had negative consequences on poor and minority individuals and their communities. This report demonstrates that the drug problem in New York cannot be resolved through what has effectively become the selective punishment of disadvantaged minority groups. In terms of reducing recidivism by promoting successful rehabilitation and re-entry into society, the Rockefeller drug laws have clearly failed New York.

Methods of Investigation

PHR and The Fortune Society conducted semi-structured interviews with fifty people convicted of drug offenses under the Rockefeller drug laws. At the time of their interviews, the subjects were all affiliated with The Fortune Society (hereafter referred to as Fortune), a not-for-profit service and advocacy organization dedicated to assisting ex-prisoners and at-risk youth through provision of a broad range of services, as well as education of the public about criminal justice issues.

The study was designed as a comprehensive sample of all intakes and active participants in Fortune's walk-in programs.[3] The research instrument included a qualitative assessment of participants' attitudes and experiences and was supplemented by a structured, quantitative survey.[4] PHR and Fortune asked respondents to discuss their childhoods and any early involvement with drugs and crime, their experiences in prison, and their efforts to re-integrate into their communities since their most recent release from prison.

Interviews were conducted between February and April, 2003. To be eligible for the study, participants had to have been released from prison between January 1, 1997 and December 2002, after serving at least one year for a drug offense conviction with no concurrent conviction for a violent offense (prior convictions, however, were not a factor in eligibility). Participants also had to be residents in the metropolitan New York City area.

The interviews were conducted by two-person teams comprised of a trained PHR interviewer and a trained peer counselor from Fortune. Interviewers used a semi-structured instrument designed for this study. The instrument obtained basic demographic data as well as chronological descriptions of the participant's socio-economic status before, during and after incarceration. Open-ended questions explored respondents' living arrangements, family situation and contacts, employment, income, education, drug use, health status and involvement in community groups.

Findings

The interviews revealed that in their lives before prison, individuals had a range of experiences and circumstances that placed them at increased risk of illegal activity. But respondents also described varying degrees of potential to contribute in family and community life as well as the labor market. Almost everyone in the study sample eventually began using drugs regularly, and consequently their social supports deteriorated.

While a few respondents said that incarceration interrupted their lifestyle of drug use, a vast majority said they did not benefit from their time in prison. Nearly all respondents noted that prison forced them to cut themselves off emotionally from their families. Long-term incarceration offered the subjects little in the way of emotional, educational or thera-

---

[3] Although the sample was not designed to be representative of the population of formerly incarcerated drug offenders, by representing a comprehensive sample of ex-prisoners associated with a key service organization it addresses many of the themes that are relevant to the broader New York population of formerly incarcerated drug offenders.

[4] This study relied on self-report for the majority of its findings and did not include verification through additional sources for most life-history information. While self-report exposes the research to potential misrepresentation by research subjects, a more likely concern in a study of this kind is that respondents will remember only some events that are not necessarily representative of their life histories. Such recall bias could exaggerate the significance of particular events and interactions and minimize the significance of others.

peutic support to help them remain crime and drug free upon re-entry into society.

Life before Prison

The people interviewed by PHR/Fortune experienced childhoods with emotional and socioeconomic deprivations that were similar to those among arrestees generally, as reported in criminal justice literature. PHR and Fortune found that, as children, nearly all of the respondents experienced economic hardships. Poverty was exacerbated by other disadvantages: nearly all subjects reported experiencing some form of deprivation during early childhood, including living in impoverished single-parent households or foster care. Participants also reported drug use in the household, an incarcerated parent and incomplete education. Nearly half of the respondents (45 percent) identified serious instability or abuse at home as children. Those respondents who had entered the child welfare system (foster care) as children reported routine abuses including corporal punishment, being locked in a room or basement, and neglect. Only 10 percent of the sample graduated high school.

In pre-prison adult life the majority of respondents described illegal work as their primary source of income. The amount of money available from street-level drug sales and related support work was significant enough that even the few who had full-time, stable legal work noted that they participated in the drug trade. Respondents clearly identified financial incentive as a primary motivation for entering the drug trade, specifically citing the desire to buy goods for themselves, their families and friends.

The people interviewed described complex relationships with family members. In many instances relations were strained by the respondents' drug use and criminal activity, but even in those families, respondents spoke about repeated efforts to maintain family structure, the importance of that foundation, and the difficulty associated with its loss.

Prison Experiences

Respondents described incarceration in upstate prisons and in New York City's jails as disorienting, isolating and brutalizing. Most frequently, people interviewed for this research reported cycles of nonviolent, petty (and occasionally serious) illegal activity followed by incarceration and an accompanying emotional toughening, followed by a return to people or an environment associated with crime and drug use, ending in re-incarceration. Sixty-nine percent of prior felony offenses were drug-related.

• Many respondents reported widespread availability of illegal drugs in city jails and in state prisons. Many, though not all, continued to use drugs in prison.

- Uniformly, respondents cited violence among inmates and frequently between inmates and guards. Indeed, many respondents, while convicted of a nonviolent crime, served portions or all of their sentences in maximum security facilities housed with inmates convicted of violent crimes, including murder and rape. Many said they witnessed abuse from correctional officers, although most said that they were not victims themselves of such abuse. The abuses they reported ranged from insults (including racial slurs), to theft and physical and sexual abuse.

- Within state prison, alleged infractions are punished by solitary confinement. Some respondents reported welcoming solitary confinement for the safety it provided from other inmates, but most described the experience as worse than being with other inmates because of the emotional and social deprivation accompanying the isolation.

- People interviewed for this research described being taken out of treatment when they were moved to different prisons, mediocre treatment, and a dearth of continuity in treatment – all of which are targeted as responsible for low success rates in the drug treatment literature.

- Most subjects questioned the utility of educational/vocational programs available to them in prison. Indeed, the quality of these programs is difficult to evaluate due to widely varying content and frequent transitions of inmates. Almost all respondents had participated in some service programming during incarceration. A few said they benefited but most did not believe the programming was useful to them. Most reported viewing these programs primarily as a way to gain favor with the parole board and pass time.

- Prison was the first place many respondents reported receiving ongoing medical care. Many discovered they were ill in prison when they developed symptoms of chronic disease, such as asthma, heart disease and, most frequently, HIV. Most noted differences in care between prisons.

- In terms of mental health, many respondents described feelings of shame, guilt and sadness because of strained or severed relationships with their families upon incarceration. A few people had come to feel that prison life was inevitable for them and even preferable to life on the streets.

- While in prison, those respondents who created families with partners in adulthood rarely were able to maintain those relationships through the prison sentence. This distance was particularly distressing for respondents who lost contact with their partner and with their children.

Re-entry into Society

PHR and Fortune found that subjects faced significant practical and emotional challenges that undermined their efforts to remain crime and drug-free. Indeed, 70 percent had attempted and failed re-entry into society more than once.

The interview subjects described a variety of sources of stress that affected their ability to abide by parole regulations, stay away from drugs and alcohol and avoid criminal activity:

- Most respondents lost their housing as a consequence of drug use, conviction or incarceration. Typically a respondent's drug use or incarceration made the subject's family reluctant to allow that person to remain in the home. In addition, following federal provisions, New York City maintains a discretion-based policy prohibiting convicted felony offenders from residing in Section 8 and other public housing for a specified (and varying based on offense) period of time after conviction. Thus, even those families that wished to maintain ties could be placed in a position of having to deny the respondent a family home.

- Few respondents had managed to find stable employment since release. The financial stress due to difficulties for those with a criminal record of finding a job exacerbated respondents' temptation to make money in the drug trade. While many described the job skills and the training programs in which they participated, most respondents appeared frustrated with their job prospects and hoped to gain new skills as a means to financial stability.

- In addition to physiological addiction to drugs, respondents found it difficult to refrain from drug use for emotional, psychological, financial, and social reasons. Upon release, respondents found that social and economic incentives to use and trade drugs remained strong. Further, many believed that their drug use was controllable despite years of addiction and treatment cycles.

- Overwhelmingly, respondents described the importance of restoring their relationships with family members. Some said that the support of their family was critical to surviving incarceration and re-entry; but many subjects described the pain of ongoing mistrust and anger from family members. Subjects experienced custody and foster care challenges associated with leaving children behind when incarcerated, and many parents interviewed spoke of repeated and partially successful efforts to restore relations and credibility with their children upon release.

Key Recommendations[5]

PHR and Fortune seek to provide practical suggestions with the long-term goal of appropriate sentencing for those arrested for drug offenses in New York State.

To New York State:

1. Grant judicial discretion.

New York should grant its judiciary the discretion to depart from statutory sentencing ranges for people convicted of nonviolent drug offenses who are not major players in drug sales operations. The laws should recognize differences in conduct, levels of danger to the community, and other factors relevant to sentencing. Judges should be able to sentence drug offenders to alternatives to incarceration programs.

2. Employ Alternatives to Incarceration.

Expand and Improve Alternatives to Incarceration: New York should increase the availability and use of alternatives to incarceration (ATIs) for people convicted of drug offenses. Nonviolent drug offenses, like simple possession, should include drug treatment and other rehabilitative services that adhere to, and seek to improve upon, best practices demonstrated in clinical literature. Prison should be the last rather than first alternative.

Don't Punish for Relapse: Health professionals in the drug treatment field accept that people will relapse during the course of their recovery. However, the courts have typically regarded relapse as a failure of rehabilitative efforts and they have punished relapse by revoking the ATI sentence and imposing an incarceratory sentence, frequently even harsher than the original prison sentence. If a person relapses while in an alternative to incarceration program, and there has been no new arrest for crime committed, there should be repeated attempts to engage the person in treatment. In addition, people should never face a sentence any more severe than they would absent the ATI program for either a drug relapse or for committing a technical violation (rule infraction) while they are in an ATI program. Finally, treatment programs should specify their policies on drug use relapse to the courts, and programs should adhere to these policies.

3. Prioritize drug treatment overall.

Substance abuse treatment should be appropriate to the assessed need of the individual and must be made available at levels that meet the demand

---

[5] An expanded list of recommendations may be found in the Conclusion of this report.

for treatment, both inside and outside of prison. The state should increase funding for drug treatment both in and outside of prisons in order to develop more accurate assessment tools as well as to increase comprehensive drug treatment programs, expand existing treatment programs and assure high levels of efficacy through staff training. An investment in treatment, while perhaps costly in the short term, is less expensive than the likely cycle of incarceration that is highly predictable with an absence of treatment.

To New York State and New York State Division of Parole

1. Provide more discretion in addressing parole violations.

A drug relapse or technical violation on parole should not automatically lead to a return to prison for the parolee who served time for a nonviolent drug offense. New York State should give the New York State Division of Parole the funds to responsibly monitor and refer parolees to rehabilitative services rather than automatically send them back to prison.

To New York State Department of Correctional Services

1. Improve drug treatment and vocational services in prison.

The New York State Department of Correctional Services must systematize and monitor treatment and vocational programs so that all staff provide consistent treatment and other services according to a program model based on research demonstrating what works, for example cognitive-behavioral therapies, particularly intensive drug treatment combined with aftercare in the community upon release. Prison vocational and drug treatment programs should follow the same standards as those outside of prison and be evaluated for outcomes. Vocational services should include career planning skills. Finally, there should always be substantial discharge planning and consistent opportunities for effective, continued treatment and programs once prisoners are released.

2. Improve Healthcare.

Ensure that prisoners receive the prevailing standard of quality health care as in the community at large and especially ensure that prisoners receive a continuity of care when they are transferred between prisons.

II. INTRODUCTION

Rockefeller Drug Laws in New York

In 1973 New York State's governor, Nelson Rockefeller, signed legislation specifying sentences for drug offenses in the state.[6] Coupled with subsequent legislation mandating higher sentences for second and third offenses[7], this initial "Rockefeller" statute has provided the basis for some of the country's most severe drug offense sentences.[8] At the extreme, judges have been required to use the Rockefeller statute to dole out life sentences to more than 500 current state prison inmates.[9] In thousands of other cases each year, people convicted of petty drug crimes are sentenced to a minimum of one year in a state prison, interrupting their lives and removing them from their families, work and communities into a brutal environment. Indeed, one scholar has used the public health measurement tool of "years of life lost" in order to compare New York's drug law incarcerations and their effects on young, minority males to catastrophic events.[10]

New York prisons are filled with people convicted of drug crimes: in 2000, close to 20,000 convicted felony offenders were sentenced to state prison and of those, 42 percent were incarcerated for drug-related offenses.[11] Meanwhile the majority of those incarcerated, in New York and nationwide, have a drug problem. In 2000, according to official sta-

---

[6] See N.Y. Penal Law 220.00-.65 (McKinney 2000), offenses involving controlled substances; id. 221.00-.55 (McKinney 2000), offenses involving marijuana; infra notes 92-103 and accompanying text on key revisions to the drug laws.

[7] See N.Y. Penal Law 70.06, known as the "Second Felony Offender Law."

[8] State penalties for violating sale and possession laws vary by substance, by the quantity of the substance sold or possessed, and by the type of offense, see The ImpacTeen Illicit Drug Team. *Illicit Drug Policies: Selected Laws from the 50 States.* Berrien Springs, MI: Andrews University, 2002. New York's penalties are among the highest, see National Criminal Justice Association. *A Guide to State Controlled Substances Acts.* Washington, DC: National Criminal Justice Association. 1991.

[9] Mark Sommer. "Cheaper to be Lenient." *The Buffalo News.* May 12, 2003.

[10] Ernest Drucker, "Population Impact of Mass Incarceration under New York's Rockefeller Drug Laws: An Analysis of Years of Life Lost." *Journal of Urban Health: Bulletin of the New York Academy of Medicine.* Vol. 79, No. 3, September 2002. Drucker compares the impact of the Rockefeller drug laws to the impact of AIDS on New York City communities, among other comparisons.

tistics, 66 percent of those incarcerated in New York were addicts; 57 percent were estimated to be addicts nationwide.[12] Other studies have found higher rates– one study estimates that 75 percent of all arrests in New York City are linked to drug or alcohol abuse.[13]

Under New York's Rockefeller drug laws, judges are required to use specific minimum sentences for drug felonies according to the weight of the drugs found in connection with the alleged offense. The judge must impose at least the minimum sentence regardless of whether she or he agrees that the sentence is appropriate. The only legal way that these sentences can be avoided upon conviction is with consent of the prosecutor. The state's association of prosecutors has most vigorously opposed repeal of the drug offense statutes. Some judges have voiced their frustration with the limits imposed on their discretion.[14]

Advocates have long argued the futility and fiscal irresponsibility of maintaining mandatory and/or lengthy prison sentences for people who need treatment for drug addiction. More recently policy makers from both New York City and elsewhere in the state have spoken about the need for reform of the Rockefeller laws. George Pataki, the current governor of New York, first called for reform in 1995, shortly after taking office.[15] To date, however, the governor has yet to reach agreement with the leaders of the New York State Legislature. Most recently, despite a heightened campaign led by music impresario Russell Simmons to pass drug law reform in fiscal year 2003, the thirty-year anniversary of the passing of the Rockefeller drug laws, the New York State Legislature again failed to find agreement with the governor's office before the summer recess.[16]

---

[11] New York State Department of Correctional Services data memo to Lindesmith Center. August 10, 2001. On file with authors. In 2000, 19,699 convicted felony offenders were sent to state prisons, of whom 8,227 were incarcerated for drug-related offenses.

[12] New York State Department of Correctional Services, *Identified Substance Abusers: December 2000* (Albany, New York, 2001): 2; Bureau of Justice Statistics Special Report, *Substance Abuse and Treatment—State and Federal Prisoners—1997*, U.S. Department of Justice, NCJ 172871(Washington, DC: 1999).

[13] National Center on Addiction and Substance Abuse at Columbia University, *Substance Abuse and Urban America: Its Impact on an American City*, New York (February, 1996), at 2.

[14] The Correctional Association of New York. *"Stupid and Irrational and Barbarous": New York Judges Speak Against the Rockefeller Drug Laws*. New York. 2001. Douglas Young, Rachel Porter & Gail Caputo. *Community Alternatives for Felony Offenders: A Preliminary Assessment*. Report to the Office of the Criminal Justice Coordinator for New York City. New York: Vera Institute of Justice. 1998.

[15] Raymond Hernandez. "In Switch, Democrats Won't Act on Pataki Plan to Ease Drug Laws" *The New York Times*. May 20, 1999. B3. Jennifer Gonnerman. "New York's Drug Law Debacle." *The Village Voice*. May 6, 1998.

[16] Al Baker. "Movement Seen for Change on Rockefeller Drug Laws." *The New York Times*. June 4, 2003. p. B6. Lynda Richardson. "Turning Hip-Hop Rhyme Against Long Jail Time." *The New York Times*. June 17, 2003. p. B2.

Reform efforts have ranged from reducing specific sentences based on offense to eliminating mandatory sentences all together. Government officials interested in reform have offered relatively restrained options, including expanding judicial discretion without eliminating prosecutorial influence. Advocacy organizations such as the Correctional Association of New York have called for a return to total judicial discretion. Further, some advocates have argued for drug decriminalization or other means of allowing utilization of the public health system rather than the criminal justice system because of the marked racial disparities in drug arrest, sentencing and incarceration.

While political debates continue about whether court officials, judges or prosecutors are best suited to determine prison sentences, the State continues to place thousands of people in its prisons each year. Some 75 percent of state inmates sentenced under Rockefeller come from New York City.[17] In keeping with informal policies, inmates are typically placed in prisons far from their homes at the beginning of their sentence,[18] resulting in little contact between inmates and their families. This isolation, coupled with correctional facilities that offer few social services, compounds the disadvantages faced by many inmates.

Arrest to Sentence to Parole in New York

Under New York State criminal law, it is illegal to possess, possess with the intention of selling or sell any illegal drug.

While any violation of these laws theoretically could result in arrest, in practice, the overwhelming majority of arrests are made in drug trade transactions that take place on the street in low-income communities. Typically, a person is arrested after an undercover police officer observes him or her buying or selling drugs or after an undercover police officer purchases drugs. Upon arrest, the defendant is taken to the police department where the case is reviewed and processed. Some defendants are let go without charges, but it is unknown how many or for what reasons.[19] Those not released are detained prior to appearing in court. Today, cases take about 24 hours before they come to court for arraignment. During this preliminary detention period the defendant is housed in a New York City jail.

As a first step, all cases, whether misdemeanor or felony, are arraigned in the state criminal court, the lower of New York's two levels of criminal law court. Initially cases are arraigned by a judge in consultation with an

---

[17] Human Rights Watch. *Collateral Casualties: Children of Incarcerated Drug Offenders in New York*. 2002.

[18] Human Rights Watch, *Collateral Casualties*.

[19] Bernard Harcourt. *Illusion of Order*. Cambridge: Harvard University Press. 2001.

assistant district attorney (the state's prosecutor) and a defense attorney (a public defender if the defendant is indigent). It is at this preliminary stage that the strengths of the case for prosecution are maintained or refuted.

Those cases that are charged as misdemeanors (which include some marijuana possession) remain in the criminal court. Meanwhile, cases that are originally charged as felony cases may stay in the criminal court if, at the discretion of the District Attorney, the charge is to be reduced to a misdemeanor. If, however, the felony charge is maintained at arraignment, in order for the prosecutor to proceed forward on the felony, the defendant has the right to be indicted by a grand jury. If the grand jury indicts, the case is transferred to the Supreme Court of New York, the higher level of the state's criminal court system. The grand jury indictment proceedings require the District Attorney's Office to present enough evidence to demonstrate that there is reasonable cause to believe the crime as charged has been committed. It is a mechanism to further ensure the integrity of the prosecution of the case. Most felony cases, however, do not go before a grand jury because the defense waives the right to do so as part of a plea agreement, discussed below.

After being indicted, the defendant may either enter into plea negotiations with the prosecutor or refuse to do so and thus go to trial. The United States Constitution establishes the right to a trial (as well as review by grand jury). However, the overwhelming majority of defendants in the United States, as well as in New York, waive this right and enter into plea negotiations with a prosecutor.[20] The plea process is based on a guilty plea by the defendant who receives, in exchange for forgoing a trial, a sentence that is likely to be less than what the defendant would receive if he/she elected to go to trial and was convicted after trial.

The plea bargaining process tends to be coercive because the sentences offered increase exponentially each time the defendant refuses to take the offer. For example, a person accused of selling less than one gram of crack (enough for one person to get high for a few hours) will typically be charged with a level B felony (Table 1)– the second highest level in the state. If the prosecutor offers a plea to a B level conviction and the defendant accepts, the defendant will likely receive a sentence of one to three years in a state prison. Should the defendant in this example refuse the plea offer (say for example, this person insists on innocence) the case will be adjourned to go to trial. The plea negotiations may continue as the adjournments carry on, depending on the prosecutor's willingness to continue with negotiations, with the offers becoming either more generous or more severe depending on the likelihood that the prosecution will win the case. In the above case, if the prosecution is optimistic about obtaining a

---

[20] E.g. Brian Reaves. *Felony Defendants in Large Urban Counties, 1998.* Washington, D.C.: Bureau of Justice Statistics. 2001.

conviction, the offer may increase from one to three years to two to four years and then from eight-and-one-third to twenty-five years.[21] These plea negotiations will be tougher for the defendant if s/he already has a felony record.

Until the defendant enters a plea or is convicted or exonerated at trial, she or he may be detained or released, a determination made at arraignment when setting bail. Bail is supposed to ensure a defendant's appearance in court taking into account the strength of the case, any prior warrant history and the seriousness of the crime. Bail is not meant to be used as a punitive measure to begin sentencing the individual before they have had their day in court. Research has demonstrated, however, that the decision to detain a defendant is one of the strongest predictors of eventual determination of plea.[22] A defendant may be released prior to determination of plea if the judge determines that s/he can be released on recognizance following the payment of bail. Bail amounts range widely and may be set at one dollar or thousands of dollars with amounts at the higher end designed to prevent the defendant from obtaining bail. Frequently, however, even the lower amounts are beyond the resources of defendants. Consequently, one of the first set of costs associated with Rockefeller drug laws are the high costs to New York City of housing detainees and transporting them to and from the courts while their cases are resolved. This process frequently lasts months due to the nature of the plea process including defense concerns, prosecutorial development, and court and attorney availability.

Sentencing under Rockefeller Drug Laws

The sentences mandated under New York's penal law are some of the most severe in the nation.[23] Indeed, when the Rockefeller drug laws were enacted in 1973, they played a major role in the introduction of mandatory minimum sentences for drug offenders in other states.[24] Under the Rockefeller drug laws, someone convicted of selling a single vial of crack

---

[21] Little research has been done on the plea process in New York or elsewhere. This example was taken from conversations with Legal Aid attorneys in Manhattan and Bronx counties. See also, Human Rights Watch. *Cruel and Usual: Disproportionate Sentences for New York Drug Offenders.* Human Rights Watch. New York. 1997.

[22] Steven Belenko, Mary Phillips, R. Demetriades, D. Eliyahu, Laura Winterfield & R. Heffernan. *Predicting Incarceration Length: Estimating the Displacement Effects of Alternatives-To-Incarceration Programs: Final Report of the Jail Displacement Study.* New York: New York City Criminal Justice Agency. 1993.

[23] National Criminal Justice Association. *A Guide to State Controlled Substances Acts.* Washington, DC: National Criminal Justice Association. 1991.

[24] Duane C. McBride, Curtis J. VanderWaal and Yvonne M. Terry-McElrath. *The Drugs-Crime Wars: Past, Present and Future Directions in Theory, Policy and Program Interventions.* ImpacTeen Research Paper No. 14. November 2001, p. 32.

must be sentenced to at least a year in prison and could be sentenced to 25 years in prison. Someone convicted of selling the same amount who had been convicted of another felony within the past ten years would be sentenced to at least 4.5 years in prison and could be sentenced to 25 years. Sentences for Class A and B drug felonies, in their maximum sentence ranges, are potentially as long or longer than sentences for a range of violent offenses such as armed robbery, rape and kidnapping.[25]

This report focuses on people who have received sentences for longer than one year (thus, felony offenses), whose most recent conviction was for a nonviolent felony drug offense in the Supreme Court of New York. Because sentences for misdemeanor offenses may be no more than one year, persons convicted of these crimes – drug and non-drug alike – typically serve their sentence in New York City, either on probation, and/or in Rikers Island, the city's principal jail.

The overwhelming majorities of inmates who are incarcerated for more than a year are sentenced in state courts and serve their sentences in state prisons. Federal courts are used only for offenses that are either specifically designated as federal crimes (such as those that take place in multiple states) or, in a small percentage of cases, crimes that could be prosecuted in either state or federal court.

New York State's penal law contains two provisions that affect all felony offenders regardless of offense: mandatory minimum sentences and extended incarceration for second felony offenders.[26] Both provisions set lower limits to incarceration terms according to type of offense and criminal history of the defendant. New York criminal law divides felonies into categories that decrease in order of severity from A (most serious) to E (least serious).

The majority of people incarcerated for drug offenses in New York state prisons were convicted under the lowest three categories of drug felony offenses.[27] In New York, for defendants who plead to low-level felonies such as C, D, and E, courts may impose "time served" plus probation in lieu of a prison sentence or incarceration of a year or less if the courts believe the indeterminate sentence range would be "unduly harsh."[28] Thus those sent to state prison as low level drug felons are most likely repeat offenders who fall under the state's harsher second felony offender law on drug sentencing or in a far less likely scenario, given that most choose to enter into plea negotiations, they insisted on going to trial, were found guilty and sentenced to prison.

---

[25] Human Rights Watch. *Cruel and Usual*.

[26] See Table 1 for New York State's mandatory incarceration by conviction.

[27] Human Rights Watch, *"Who Goes to Prison for Drug Offenses?" A Human Rights Watch Update*, March 18, 1999. http://www.hrw.org/campaigns/drugs/ny-drugs.htm

[28] NY Penal Code Section 70.00 (4).

TABLE 1:
Length of Mandatory Incarceration by Conviction Charge in New York

Felony Level	Minimum Sentence	Maximum Sentence
A1		
Possession (4 + ounces)	15 – 25 years	Life in prison
Sale (2 + ounces)	15 – 25 years	Life in prison
A2		
Possession (2 + ounces)	3 – 8.5 years	Life in prison
Sale (.5 + ounces)	3 – 8.5 years	Life in prison
B		
Possession of any amount with intent to sell	1 year – up to 1/3 of max.	3 – 25 years
Possession of .5 + ounces	1 year – up to 1/3 of max.	3 – 25 years
Sale of any amount	1 year – up to 1/3 of max.	3 – 25 years
C		
Possession 1/8+ ounces	1 year – up to 1/3 of max.*	3 – 15 years
D		
Possession of 500+ mg.	1 year – up to 1/3 of max.*	3 – 7 years
Sale of any amount	1 year – up to 1/3 of max.*	3 – 7 years

* New York Penal Law (70.00) grants judicial authority to impose a sentence of one year or less for some C and D felonies.

The terms of incarceration determined by New York's legislative and executive branches took sentencing discretion away from judges who were permitted to grant less severe sentences prior to the establishment of mandatory minimums. All remaining discretion is left in the hands of prosecutors at the point of determining prosecution charge. The minimum sentence mandates give state prosecutors the power to set the punitive jeopardy facing the defendant because it is only through establishing the offense charge that sentences remain discretionary. Once the prosecuting charge is established, the judge may not depart from the minimum sentence stipulated for that offense unless the prosecutor agrees to reduce the charge.

Under the Rockefeller statute, the level of the offense is determined by the weight of the drug. Meanwhile, the length of the sentence is determined by two factors: the weight of the drug and whether or not the defendant has a previous felony conviction within ten years. Thus the nature of the offense, the circumstances under which the offense took

TABLE 2:
Sentencing Range under Second Felony Offender Laws

Felony Level	Minimum	Maximum
A	6 – 12.5 years	Life imprisonment
B	4.5 – 12.5 years	9 – 25 years
C	3 – 7.5 years	6 – 15 years
D	2 – 3.5 years	4 – 7 years
E	1.5 – 3 years	3 – 4 years

place, and the character and lifestyle of the defendant are not reflected in the length of a sentence.

Sale or possession of any amount of specific illegal substances (including narcotic drugs) can be classified as a B, C, D or E felony. Sale of two ounces or possession of four ounces of a narcotic is classified as an A1-level felony, the most serious in the state's penal code, and sale of one half an ounce or possession of two ounces is classified as an A2-level felony. While sale of marijuana may result in state prison incarceration, the Rockefeller drug laws deal primarily with the possession and sale of narcotics, primarily cocaine, its cheaper derivative crack, and heroin, which are the most common drugs involved in felonies in New York. Table 1 provides the minimum and maximum sentences by felony offense level according to New York State Penal Law for Controlled Substances (Section 220).

In addition to mandatory minimums for first-time felony offenders, the State mandated longer prison sentences for felonies committed by people who had already been convicted of a felony, the Second Felony Offenders laws. Table 2 details the minimum sentence by felony level that these laws mandate.

Thus a person who had been convicted of a low-level felony offense (e.g. a D-level offense) for drug possession eight years ago, who is convicted of a second D-level drug possession offense, must be sentenced to at least two to three and a half years in state prison. Should the same person be convicted of a higher drug charge, for example a B-level offense, the judge in the case is required to sentence the person convicted of the charge to a minimum of four and a half to twelve and a half years in prison even if the first conviction was for a low-level offense. This is the same minimum amount of time that a judge is required to use to sentence an offender convicted of rape, robbery and a host of other violent crimes.[29] Another factor, the type of drug, is also used to distinguish between low-level and other offenses.

---

[29] New York Penal Law, Section 70.

"Fifteen Years to Life": The Case of Anthony Papa[30]

Anthony Papa's case has become well known as an example of egregious, lengthy sentences served by persons convicted of nonviolent drug offenses under the Rockefeller drug laws. In 1985, Anthony Papa was charged as an A1 felony offender and sentenced to 15 years to life for the delivery of 4.5 ounces of cocaine. He was 30 years old.

Prior to his arrest, Papa was the owner of a small car radio and alarm installation business in the Bronx. He had had two run-ins with the law for disorderly conduct, but no drug charges. During a slow period for his business, he was desperately in need of money to pay his bills when a bowling teammate offered him a deal. Papa could earn $500 just by delivering an envelope containing 4.5 ounces of cocaine. Papa agreed, not knowing that his bowling "buddy" was an informant for the police trying to reduce his punishment for three prior drug offenses. Papa was arrested upon handing the envelope to an undercover officer.

On the advice of his attorney, Papa refused a plea bargain and went to trial, where the undercover officers testified that they had never seen Papa before in their work in narcotics. Nevertheless, he was found guilty and sentenced to prison for 15 years under the Rockefeller drug laws and was sent to Sing Sing, a maximum security prison.

At the time of his arrest, Papa was married with one daughter. His wife divorced him. During his years of imprisonment, Papa earned three degrees and became a prominent artist, generating acclaim in the art world. Following widespread attention to his case through his artwork, Governor Pataki granted him clemency on Christmas Eve, 1996 and he was released on parole in January 1997 after serving 12 years. Papa founded Mothers of the New York Disappeared, an advocacy organization that works for drug-law reform.

Parole

Finally, a sentence in New York State is indeterminate, i.e. there is a range of incarceration imposed with a mandatory minimum and mandatory maximum sentence. If a defendant serves his or her minimum sentence range and is released, s/he usually remains under criminal justice supervision for the maximum period, under parole.

Parole is likely to be granted at some point after the prisoner has served the minimum sentence. However, whether parole is granted is determined by members of the New York State Board of Parole, which consists of up

---

[30] Adapted from Families Against Mandatory Minimums (FAMM) case files. Papa wrote a book about his experiences, *"Fifteen Years to Life": How I Painted My Way to Freedom* (Feral House, forthcoming 2004).

to 19 people appointed by the governor, and is not guaranteed to an inmate. Parole may be denied for no reason or for reasons that appear capricious or unfair to the inmate; decisions may be left unexplained.

Once an inmate is released on parole, s/he must adhere to the extensive regulations of conditional release, for example, making appointments with the parole officer, continuing to abstain from drugs including from alcohol and staying within the state and away from other parolees. Failure to observe these strictures can result in return to state custody for the amount of time that remained on the maximum sentence when the inmate was released. Parole officer caseloads tend to be high, but it is not clear how this may affect officer willingness to return a parolee to custody. There is little quantitative research on the nature of parole violation; however it is clear that parole violations, both for rule infractions ("technical") and for new arrests, account for an increasing percent of prison admissions, about 31 percent in New York State.[31]

The Social and Economic Effects of the Rockefeller Drug Laws

New York State's Prison Population

While the total number of inmates in New York's state prison system has declined slightly in the past year, the state continues to spend billions incarcerating primarily African-American and Latino persons, mainly for drug offenses. Drug convictions accounted for around 40 percent of the state's new commitments to state prison over the last few years.[32] Under the Rockefeller drug laws, the state has increased the number of inmates and has thereby also increased the amount of money needed to house and supervise the burgeoning inmate population. Consequently, the financial burden levied by the state's criminal justice system on New York state taxpayers has skyrocketed. The costs associated with keeping an inmate in state prison for a year are approximately $30,000. A study conducted by two advocacy organizations, the Justice Policy Institute and the Correctional Association, found that New York State increased spending on prison construction and administration by 76 percent between 1988 and 1998, culminating in the state spending $1.6 billion on its prison system in 1998.[33]

The high costs associated with incarceration have forced states nation-

---

[31] Timothy Hughes, Doris Wilson & Allen Beck. *Trends in State Parole, 1999-2000* Washington, D.C.: Bureau of Justice Statistics. 2001.

[32] The Correctional Association of New York, "Trends in New York State Prison Commitments," Correctional Association, February 2004.

[33] Robert Gangi, Vincent Schiraldi & Jason Ziedenberg. *New York State of Mind?: Higher Education vs. Prison Funding in the Empire State, 1988-1998*. Washington, D.C. & New York: The Justice Policy Institute & The Correctional Association of New York. 1997

wide to find ways to relieve the cost burden of the mandatory minimum sentences.[34] In New York, a new law[35] allows certain inmates serving indeterminate sentences for non-violent felonies (excluding class A1 felony drug and non drug offenders) to earn a certificate for good behavior. This makes them eligible for a program called "presumptive release," which means that they can be automatically released to parole supervision when they reach their parole eligibility date. In addition, another new law allows people incarcerated under A1 felony drug charges to be eligible for early release credit at twice the merit time available to other inmates (they were previously ineligible for any release credit).[36] These two new laws are "back-end" sentence adjustments at the discretion of the office of the corrections commissioner rather than outright drug law sentencing reforms, and the implementation remains to be seen.

Disproportionate Impact on Low-Income and Minority Communities

The overwhelming majority of people who are convicted of drug offenses in New York and throughout the country are African-American or Latino and are represented by public defenders. In 1980 the New York State Department of Corrections received a total of 886 new prison commitments for drug-related offenses. Of those, 32 percent were Caucasian, 38 percent were African-American and 29 percent were Latino. In 1992, when the state saw its largest number of commitments for drug-related offenses, 5 percent were Caucasian, 50 percent were African-American and 44 percent were Latino. In 2000, the New York state prison system received 8,227 new commitments for drug-related offenses, of which only 6 percent were Caucasian, 53 percent were African-American, and 40 percent were Latino. [37] Thus, in 2000, of the persons newly committed to the New York State prison system for drug-related offenses, 93 percent were African-American or Latino. African-Americans and Latinos make up about 30 percent of New York State's population.[38]

---

[34] Fox Butterfield, "With Cash Tight, States Reassess Long Jail Terms," *New York Times,* November 10, 2003.

[35] New York Correction Law, Section 806. The presumptive release program is not a right and decisions are at the discretion of the office of the commissioner of New York's Department of Correctional Services.

[36] New York Correction Law, Section 803.

[37] New York State Department of Correctional Services data memo to Lindesmith Center. August 10, 2001. On file with authors. In addition, PHR obtained NYS Department of Correctional Services statistics for persons under custody for drug offenses as of December 31, 2003: of 17,081 total, 15,809 (92.5 percent) were African-American or Hispanic and 1,025 were white (6 percent).

[38] US Census Bureau, *State and County QuickFacts: New York.* See http://quickfacts.census.gov/qfd/states/36000.html. Accessed March 15, 2004.

While the vast majority of people incarcerated under the Rockefeller drug laws are minority men, the drug laws also have had a large impact on women, especially minority women. While women are a small percentage of prison inmates—they make up less than five percent of New York's prison population—the Rockefeller drug laws have contributed enormously to the increase in the number of women in New York's state prisons. According to the Correctional Association of New York, when New York State enacted the Rockefeller drug laws in 1973, 400 women were incarcerated in New York State prisons; and as of January 1, 2002, more than 3,100 women were incarcerated.[39] Almost the entire increase (91 percent) in women sentenced to prison from 1986 to 1995 was a result of drug offenses.[40] In January 2001, for example, over 90 percent of women under custody for a drug offense were women of color: 54 percent were African-American and 37 percent were Latina.[41]

While the nature and reasons for racial disparities are debated, policing efforts that target minority communities are clearly responsible for higher arrest rates in those neighborhoods. Police initiatives such as Operation TNT in the 1980s and Operation Weed and Seed from the 1990s used expanded police forces in defined areas. These initiatives target neighborhoods for intensive policing. Police saturate a discrete area within the city in an effort to eradicate the drug market operating there. Techniques such as "stop and frisk" to detect drug possession and "buy and bust" undercover work to catch drug sales target petty and other drug activity that takes place in public places. For both logistical and strategic reasons, the police department maintains no such commensurate effort at targeting petty drug offending that occurs indoors. Because of the development of delivery services in New York, people who can afford it can obtain drugs by using a telephone or pager to contact a drug supplier and do not have to go onto the street with drugs or in order to buy drugs. The drug transactions that occur on the street are generally conducted by low-income people living in communities that are primarily non-white.[42] Consequently, most arrests made in New York's drug war are of non-white, low-income people.

Nationally-collected arrest data demonstrates that drug sales leading to arrests in New York are more likely to take place on the street than in other parts of the country. According to recent Arrestee Drug Abuse Monitoring data (2000), 92 percent of crack cocaine sales and 84 percent of

---

[39] From the Correctional Association of New York's Women in Prison Project: "Women in Prison Fact Sheet," March 2002.

[40] "Women in Prison Fact Sheet."

[41] "Women in Prison Fact Sheet."

[42] Tonry. 1995.

heroin sales in Manhattan during the survey period took place outside.[43] Of those arrested in the sample, only 10 percent were white. The arrestees showed a clear need for drug treatment: 93 percent of those arrested for drug-crimes tested positive for drug use at arrest and more than three-quarters said they needed treatment (though of those, two-thirds said they could not get treatment because they had no insurance).[44]

These statistics demonstrate the problems posed by drug markets in New York's minority communities. Most people arrested for drug crimes are African-American or Latino and use drugs as opposed to merely selling. The neighborhoods affected by these arrests are also affected by drug dealing and drug use in public places. Many community activists struggle to develop ways to eradicate drug market activity without leading to the incarceration of significant numbers of their members. In addition, these raids do not necessarily affect the supply chain. The sweeps take a few foot-soldiers off the street, but the trade either moves elsewhere and/or others are willing to take the place of those arrested.

Meanwhile, in communities such as Washington Heights in northern Manhattan, Bushwick in Brooklyn and Hunts Point in the Bronx, there is little concentrated public spending to foster economic development and few jobs. Employment that pays more than the minimum wage or that offers benefits is especially scarce.[45] This problem is exacerbated by a history of incarceration, particularly for those who drop out of high school.[46] In these neighborhoods the drug trade can be a more accessible and lucrative source of income than legal employment. It is also in these neighborhoods that the city targets anti-drug law enforcement, and it is, therefore, from these neighborhoods that the state draws its prison population. According to one analysis, fully 75 percent of New York State inmates come from seven low-income New York City neighborhoods.[47]

Of course, low-income and minority neighborhoods are home to people who have never committed a crime of any sort, who oppose drug dealing, and who complain that their streets are inadequately policed. Some research, however, has indicated that the strictest drug laws in the country

---

[43] *Arrestee Drug Abuse Monitoring: Annual Report 2000.* Washington D.C.: National Institute of Justice. 2003.

[44] *Ibid.* See also Jerome Skolnick, "Drug Enforcement, Violent Crime and the Minimization of Harm" in Edward Rubin, ed. *Minimizing Harm.* Oxford, UK: Westview Press, 1999.

[45] Loic Wacquant. Deadly Symbiosis: When Ghetto and Prison Meet and Mesh. *Punishment and Society.* Vol. 2. 2000. Katherine Newman *No Shame in My Game: The Working Poor in the Inner City.* New York: Russell Sage Foundation & Knopf. 1999.

[46] Bruce Western, Becky Pettit and Josh Guetzkow. "Black Economic Progress in the Era of Mass Imprisonment" in, Marc Mauer and Meda Chesney-Lind, eds. *Invisible Punishment: The Collateral Consequences of Mass Imprisonment.* New York: The New Press. 2002.

[47] Edwin Ellis. *The Nontraditional Approach to Criminal Justice and Social Justice.* New York: The Community Justice Center. 1993.

have virtually no impact on the safety of those communities.[48] Further, when a young man or woman is arrested in one of these neighborhoods, his or her family, friends, partner and employer all remain. Nationally, a young black man has approximately a one in four chance of being incarcerated in a state or federal prison in his lifetime.[49]

Social scientists have pointed out that the communities left behind after incarceration both suffer the loss of significant portions of their population and are further structurally affected by legislation such as the Adoption and Safe Families Act of 1997,[50] which imposes additional "invisible" punishments on ex-prisoners and their families when they return home.[51] These invisible punishments include restricted voting rights, ineligibility for public housing, limitations on child custody rights, and other restrictions on the ex-prisoner's ability to integrate with society such as denial of federal grants for higher education and ineligibility for certain jobs. When large numbers of people in a community are subject to these restrictions, the entire community infrastructure is weakened.[52]

A Link between Rockefeller Drug Laws and Upstate Development?

Inmates predominately come from New York City and are African-American or Latino, but most prisons are built in upstate New York counties and are staffed by people residing in these counties (mainly white, rural populations). New York State has a total of 71 prisons, and some reform advocates have pointed out that of the 41 prisons built in New York since1983, 40 were built in districts represented by Republicans in the

---

[48] Joint Committee on Drug Law Evaluation. *The Nation's Toughest Drug Law: Evaluating the New York Experience.* Washington, D.C.: The Bar Association of the City of New York and the Drug Abuse Council. 1978.

[49] Thomas Bonczar and Allen Beck. *Lifetime Likelihood of Going to State or Federal Prison.* Washington D.C.: Bureau of Justice Statistics, U.S. Department of Justice. 1997. The median sentence length for a first incarceration in a state or federal prison was 60 months. See also, Marc Mauer. *Young Black Men and the Criminal Justice System: A Growing National Problem.* Washington, D.C.: The Sentencing Project. 1990.

[50] The Adoption and Safe Families Act of 1997 (Public Law 105-89).

[51] Loic Waquant. "Negative Social Capital: State Breakdown and Social Distribution in America's Urban Core." *Netherlands Journal of Housing and Built Environment.* Vol. 13, no. 1. 1998. p. 25-39. John Hagan. "Returning Captives of the American War on Drugs: Issues of Community and Family Recovery." *Crime & Delinquency.* Vol. 47, no. 3. 2001. p. 352-367. Jeremy Travis. "Invisible Punishment: An Instrument of Social Exclusion" in Marc Mauer and Meda Chesney-Lind, eds. *Invisible Punishment: The Collateral Consequences of Mass Imprisonment.* New York: The New Press. 2002.

[52] James Lynch and William Sabol. *Did Getting Tough on Crime Pay?* Washington D. C.: The Urban Institute. 1997. Todd Clear, Dina Rose & Judith Ryder. " Incarceration and the Community: The Problem of Removing and Returning Offenders." *Crime & Delinquency.* Vol. 47, no.3. 2001. p. 335-351.

New York State Legislature – it is those representatives who have consistently supported strict and prolonged prison sentences.[53]

Given the distance between these upstate counties and the New York City neighborhoods that are over-represented in state prisons, some have alleged that public safety concerns may not be at the heart of this legislative support for strict sentencing. Rather, laws that explicitly result in more and longer prison sentences provide the path to economic development in these rural upstate districts that are struggling to maintain jobs and local economies in the wake of the collapse or relocation of industries that historically sustained these communities. As such, many communities now depend on the jobs and accompanying income that come with new prisons.[54]

In addition, the media and advocates for drug law reforms have pointed out that almost all (over 90 percent) of New York State's prisoners are incarcerated in upstate New York; they cannot vote yet they are counted for census and political representation purposes in those upstate counties.[55]

---

[53] Lisa Freeman & Robert Gangi. *Following the Dollars: Where New York State Spends Its Prison Moneys*. New York: The City Project. 2000. See also, Eric Schlosser. "The Prison Industrial Complex" *The Atlantic Monthly*. December 1998.

[54] Peter Wagner. *Racial Disparities in the 'Great Migration' to Prison Call for Reassessing Crime Control Policy*. The Prison Policy Initiative. 2001. http://www.prisonpolicy.org/articles/upr100701.shtml

[55] Peter Wagner. *Importing Constituents: Prisoners and Political Clout in New York*. The Prison Policy Initiative. 2002. http://www.prisonpolicy.org/importing/importing.shtml. See also Clyde Haberman. "Census Time: Will the Felon Please Rise." *New York Times*. April 4, 2000. B1.

One Woman's Story: DS

DS's story typifies struggles with addiction, its effects on families, and the potential of treatment programs as alternatives to incarceration.

DS is a 47-year-old African-American woman. At the time of the interview, she had served two short prison sentences for felony drug offenses, once for a sale in 1992 (1.5 years of a 1.5-3 year sentence served) and the other for a felony sale in 2001 (3 months of a 4.5-9 year sentence served before she "programmed out" into a residential treatment center for 12 months).

She came from a "huge family" of thirteen kids. "I'm the baby. I was a spoiled brat. I got whatever I wanted when I wanted it.... I grew up with two brothers. They got into a lot of trouble. My mother was a single parent. My father died when I was six. My mother and I had a beautiful relationship. She tried to steer me...." But, "I wanted to be a follower, not a leader. I followed, to be like kids at school, and my brothers. Robbing, stealing, using heroin and pills. I got pregnant in the 11th grade. I got married to the father at 18." DS's husband was in the military and was posted abroad; they had two children and moved back to New York in the late 1970s.

DS says, "My husband got on drugs in the military. He was 34 when he started using." While DS was working after they returned to New York, her husband lost his job. She came home one night and he was there with an addict. "I said, 'I can't have this.' And I put him out."

Four years later, "I met a guy. We started talking at the corner. I got into a relationship with him. He was selling crack and turned me onto it. After a while he wouldn't give me anymore and I had to get it on my own. In October, 1983 I got fired from Citibank. My kids were uneasy. They asked, 'Mommy, why don't you get us things anymore?' Or 'why do this or that anymore?' At Christmas I didn't get them what I was supposed to. I had to move in with my sister. She did it for the kids.'" Of that time, she says, "When I was high, I felt okay. But when I came down, the guilt set in."

DS hooked up with a dealer and agreed to sell for him, "70-30. He takes 70 [percent], I take 30." She began engaging in sex for money, and said, "I used to hate myself for it. The kids would ask, 'Mommy, when are you going to go back to work?'. I used to look good in the morning but now my daughter started asking what was wrong with me."

DS continued to use and sell through the 1990s. "In '98 I sent them [the kids] to my mother in New Orleans. She wanted them because I was druggin'. They were sad but happy to go because I wasn't doing anything for them. My kids, brothers and sisters, they were disappointed in me. My sisters were there for them [the kids]. They told my sister, 'Mommy is f——g up.'"

Of her addiction, DS says, "Because I was using drugs, I needed to make more and more money. The more you sell and smoke, the more money and drugs you need..... When I was using, I wasn't thinking about the future. It was just day by day."

During her first incarceration, DS participated in ASAT [a part-time drug education and treatment program operated by the Department of Correctional Services] and was granted work release after serving 1.5 years of 1.5 to 3 year sentence for criminal sale. Of prison, "It was a stressful life. Not all the CO's were good. Not all were bad. It took a while to get used to being locked up. I learned to mind my own business. One girl, she was aggressive. I had to fight her, had to show I was strong. I spent 13 days in the hole for that [solitary confinement]. After that, they left me alone." Despite the ASAT treatment program, DS says she knew, "Once I got out, I was gonna use again. Nothing about being in prison made me think about stopping drugs." Indeed, "The day I got out, as soon as I got out, I took the money I got when I was released, bought some crack on the street, went upstairs and smoked it."

"Still drugging" after release, DS serving short turnaround stays in jail for misdemeanors, including prostitution and trespassing. "I was an addict. When you're an addict you don't think about future anything. It's just about now."

DS lived with her daughter. One day in 2001, DS's daughter told her she "'wasn't standing for it anymore.' My daughter kicked me out and said you have to go to a [drug treatment] program and don't come back here 'til you get your life together." I didn't go. I was going to but I thought, 'one more hit before I go.' I met a guy, got high, and got busted."

DS received a 4.5 – 9 year suspended prison sentence because she says she was lucky and this time had "a good attorney, a pro bono attorney, who got me into the program." Her second prison sentence was only 3 months because DS was released into a mandated residential treatment program, PSI. DS did well in the program and "got to be a coordinator." She said re-joining her family has motivated her to do well. If she were to graduate from the program, this would preclude her 4.5-9 year suspended sentence. She has a strong sense of accomplishment.

"I have goals now. To go to school to be a sonogram technician. To be a role model for the program. PSI gave me all that. Through therapy I know what my 'triggers' are for taking drugs." Knowing these triggers, she says, she can find other ways of dealing with them, alternatives to taking drugs. The support of the group she is in helps a great deal, she says.

Having experienced both prison and a residential treatment program, DS says, "I don't think jail solves anything. Therapy, programs help with your addiction. They help you learn why you used drugs in the first place." She said, "If you're an addict, jail is not the answer. Programs, therapy, they are the answer."

III. FINDINGS

Methods of Investigation

PHR and The Fortune Society conducted semi-structured interviews with fifty people formerly incarcerated under the Rockefeller drug laws. The research was designed to elicit narratives regarding individual experiences prior to the first arrest, once in prison, and after release.

At the time of their interviews, the subjects were all affiliated with The Fortune Society, a not-for-profit service and advocacy organization dedicated to assisting ex-prisoners and at-risk youth through a broad range of services, as well as educating the public about criminal justice issues.

The study was designed as a comprehensive sample of all intakes and active participants in Fortune's walk-in programs. The research instrument included a qualitative assessment of participants' attitudes and experiences and was supplemented by structured, quantitative questions as well.

Although the sample was not designed to be representative of ex-prisoners who were incarcerated for drug offenses in New York, the life stories of the participants illustrate many of the themes that are relevant to the broader New York population of formerly incarcerated drug offenders. The sample may not be representative of the total population of people who were sentenced to prison for drug-related crimes because it is taken entirely from the active client base of a direct service organization. Accessing services may be an indicator of a higher level of functioning, but it is not possible to confirm this.

In addition, as with much social science research, this study relied on self-report for the majority of its findings and did not include verification through additional sources for most life-history information. While self-report exposes the research to potential misrepresentation by research subjects, a more likely concern in a study of this kind is that respondents will remember only some events that are not necessarily representative of their life histories. Such recall bias could exaggerate the significance of particular events and interactions and minimize the significance of others.

Beginning February 24, 2003, all new intakes into the agency's walk-in programs were screened by Fortune for eligibility for inclusion in the study. At the same time, all eligible active clients in the same programs were recruited for the study. Potential participants were recruited based on the following eligibility criteria:

- Most recent conviction was for a drug offense

- Sentenced to and served at least one year of this conviction in a New York state prison

- Released from prison January 1, 1997 or later, but at least three months prior to the study start date

- No concurrent conviction for a violent offense

- Resident of the New York City metro area

All interviews were conducted between February and April, 2003 by teams of two researchers. Each of these teams consisted of one of four trained lead interviewers assisted by one of three co-interviewers who were former Fortune clients, in recovery from substance use themselves, and who served as peer counselors in Fortune's programs. Because the co-interviewers shared life experiences with the interviewees, they added to the lead interviewer's ability to elicit and interpret responses. The interviewers were trained in how to administer semi-structured surveys consisting of open-ended questions, and all interviewers participated in a day-long training and preparation session.

PHR and Fortune developed a semi-structured instrument that assessed life experiences prior to, during and after prison (see Appendix III). The pre-prison portion of the interview explored chronological descriptions of the participant's socio-economic status, living arrangements, family social relationships, employment and other income, education, health status, drug use, criminal activity and involvement in community groups. The section about prison experience included descriptions of prison-based program involvement, physical and mental health, social and institutional relationships and perception of abuse. The reentry section of the interview examined housing and employment patterns, family and social relationships, lingering effects of imprisonment on mental and physical condition and drug use and criminal activity.

This study was reviewed and approved by an independent, Physicians for Human Rights ethics review board (ERB) of five individuals with expertise in bioethics, health, human rights and prison issues. In reviewing the research, the ERB was guided by the relevant process provisions of Title 45 of the US Code of Federal Regulations,[56] and complied with the Declaration of Helsinki, as revised in 2000.[57] All data were kept confidential and data stored in databases was stripped of identifiers. Potential sub-

---

[56] United States Department of Health and Human Services. Title 45 CFR Part 46, Protection Of Human Subjects. Available at: http://ohsr.od.nih.gov/mpa/45cfr46.php3. Accessed April 4, 2003.

jects were assured that participation was not required and would not assist them in any way other than the one time receipt of a $50 gift certificate at a major clothing retailer, which was determined by the ERB to be appropriate compensation for the time spent in the interview. Prior to the interview, participants were informed about the research and asked if they were certain they wanted to continue. Verbal and written informed consent was obtained from all participants. During the interviews, PHR and Fortune interviewers took extensive notes and, when prior consent was given, the interviews were recorded. To protect confidentiality, the research subjects are referred to by non-identifying initials in this report.

The interviews varied in length but typically lasted two hours. If a respondent wished to take a break, or if the researchers felt the respondent was unable to focus, the interviews were interrupted for a few minutes and then continued.

PHR interviewers wrote up their extensive notes, indicating information gathered on the themes in the instrument. A specialist in prison research analyzed the interviews for content, patterns and frequency, contextualized findings and drafted the report, which was then reviewed by the interviewers.

Characteristics of the Sample

The people interviewed were primarily male (80 percent) and African-American (59 percent) or Latino (29 percent). Most respondents (90 percent) reported that they were not currently married. Three quarters of those interviewed had children.

In keeping with criminal sentencing in New York and throughout the country, the overwhelming majority of people (96 percent) interviewed waived their right to a jury trial and were sentenced according to plea negotiations. Almost all respondents either were on or had completed parole. Respondents described prior extensive histories of incarceration. Seventy percent of the sample had committed prior felonies and most of the prior felony offenses were drug-related. With an average of 41 years of age, respondents had spent an average of almost half (46 percent) of their adult lives incarcerated. Drug-related prison time accounted for an average of 78 percent of their time served, or more than one third (35 percent) of their adult lives.

People interviewed for this study were more likely to be employed after prison than before, see Table 5 (Employment and Income). Forty-four percent of the sample reported being employed prior to going to prison, while

---

[57] World Medical Association. Declaration of Helsinki: Ethical Principles for Medical Research Involving Human Subjects [5th rev.] Edinburgh, Scotland: World Medical Association; 2000.

TABLE 3:
Socio-demographic Characteristics

	No. (%)
Gender (n=50)	
Male	40 (80%)
Female	10 (20%)
Age (years), mean ± se (range) (n=49)	41 ± 1 (23-62)
Race/Ethnicity (n=49)	
African-American	29 (59%)
Hispanic/Latino	14 (29%)
Other	4 (8%)
Caucasian	2 4%)
Marital Status (n=49)	
Single	29 (59%)
Divorced	6 (12%)
Separated	6 (12%)
Married	5 (10%)
Other	2 (4%)
Widowed	1 (2%)
Education (years of school), mean ± se (range) (n=49)	12 ± .3 (7-16)
Number of Children (n=49)	
0	13 (27%)
1	12 (25%)
2-4	20 (40%)
5-7	4 (8%)
Knows about special process to register to vote (n=46)	
Yes	20 (44%)
No	26 (56%)

64 percent were employed after prison. Employment is a condition of parole, so this increase is not surprising.

It is important, however, to note the difference here between the quantitative and qualitative findings of this research. The qualitative data suggests that the 64 percent figure is an optimistic assessment including temporary, under-the-table, and unstable employment as well as fulltime, permanent positions, which the qualitative data indicate are rare in the sample. The decrease in income from an average of more than $2,000 per month to $434 per month demonstrate the depressed wages which job seekers with criminal records must accept.

Tables 6 and 7 demonstrate other changes in the sample after incarceration. Table 6 shows that incarceration was likely to negatively affect support of children. Table 3, above, demonstrated that 75 percent of the respondents had children, but Table 6 shows that 68 percent of the sample

TABLE 4:
Criminal Justice Information

	No. (%)
Most Recent Offense (n=50)	
B: 220.39 Criminal sale of controlled substance-3rd deg.	14 (28%)
C: 220.34 Criminal sale of controlled substance-4th deg.	10 (20%)
D: 220.31 Criminal sale of controlled substance-5th deg.	9 (18%)
D: 220.06 Criminal possession of controlled substance-5th deg.	5 (10%)
C: 220.09 Criminal possession of controlled substance-4th deg	(8%)
B: 220.16 Criminal possession of controlled substance-3rd deg	3(6%)
AII: 220.4 Criminal sale of controlled substance-2nd deg.	2 (4%)
E: 105.10 Conspiracy in the 4th deg.	1 (2%)
A1: 220.43 Criminal sale of controlled substance-1st deg	1 (2%)
C: 220.65 Criminal sale of prescription for controlled substance	1 (2%)
Most recent sentence was a result of … (n=48)	
Plea bargain	46 (96%)
Guilty verdict	2 (4%)
Current Parole Status (n=48)	
Currently on parole	32 (67%)
Completed parole	15 (31%)
Never paroled	1 (2%)
Total # of Felony Offenses (n=47)	
1	14 (30%)
2	11 (23%)
3	10 (21%)
4	2 (4%)
5	7 (15%)
6	3 (6%)
Lifetime Total Time Served for Other Offenses (months) mean ± se (range) (n=49)	87 ± 9 (12-252)
Time served for prior felonies plus for most recent offense (years), mean ± (range), (n=45)	10.5 (yrs) ± 6.4 (2-27)

did not support children – indicating that only 32 percent of the sample supported children prior to incarceration. Predictably, given the income findings above, that number dropped even further after release from prison to 19 percent. Table 7 demonstrates a similar decline in participation in some community-based activities, much of which can presumably be attributed to an aging-out phenomena but perhaps also due to the alienating experience of the prison environment, where respondents often cited the need to keep to themselves. The increase in religious activity from 28 percent before incarceration to 46 percent after is likely attributable to

TABLE 5:
Employment and Income (before and after prison)

	No. (%)	No. (%)
Employed?	*Before prison (n=48)*	*After prison (n=31)*
Yes	21 (44%)	17 (64%)
Income ($), mean ± se (range)	*Before prison (n=32)*	*After prison (n=27)*
	2,888 ± 922 (0-24,000)	434 ± 71 (0-1,100)

TABLE 6:
Children and dependents (before and after prison)

	No. (%)	No. (%)
# Children supported	Before prison (n=43)	After prison (n=46)
None	29 (67%)	37 (80%)
1	5 (12%)	4 (9%)
2	7 (16%)	4 (9%)
3	1 (2%)	1 (2%)
4	1 (2%)	0
# Dependents supported	Before prison (n=41)	After prison (n=43)
None	25 (61%)	36 (84%)
1	4 (10%)	3 (7%)
2	8 (20%)	2 (5%)
3	3 (7%)	2 (5%)
4	1 (2%)	0

TABLE 7:
Participation in social groups (before and after prison)

	No. (%)	No. (%)
Religious group	*Before prison (n=49)*	*After prison (n=47)*
	14 (29%)	22 (47%)
School	*Before prison (n=49)*	*After prison (n=48)*
	14 (29%)	10 (21%)
Sports	*Before prison (n=48)*	*After prison (n=47)*
	18 (38%)	5 (11%)
Neighborhood assoc	*Before prison (n=48)*	*After prison (n=48)*
	8 (17%)	7 (15%)

the religious content of much drug treatment, notably Alcoholics Anonymous and Narcotics Anonymous groups. In addition, the increase in religious activity relates to the acquisition of religion as a coping mechanism including increased contact with outsiders (such as the clergy) while incarcerated.

Voting rights vary by state. Most states bar those in prison and those on parole or probation from voting.[58] (Only Maine and Vermont allow prisoners to vote). New York bars prisoners and parolees from voting. While slightly more than half of the sample (60 percent) had registered to vote prior to incarceration, that number fell precipitously to 29 percent after release from prison. The number of people in the sample who voted prior to and after prison varies even more: 45 percent prior to incarceration and only 17 percent after release.

These findings on voting participation suggest that the impact of incarceration and parole on communities is likely to have a cumulative effect on the extent to which the communities are represented politically.

TABLE 8:
Voting Status (before and after prison)

	No. (%)	No. (%)
Registered to vote	*Before prison (n=47)*	*After prison (n=49)*
	28 (60%)	14 (29%)
Voted	*Before prison (n=47)*	*After prison (n=48)*
	21 (45%)	8 (17%)

[58] Abby Goodnough. "Disenfranchised Florida Felons Struggle to Regain Their Rights." *The New York Times*. March 28, 2004, A1.

IV. LIFE BEFORE PRISON

Sociological research has examined the impact of childhood experiences of deprivation on the development of adult norms[59] and criminal justice literature has documented the prevalence of childhood emotional, socio-economic, and physical disadvantage among arrestees.[60]

Childhood experiences were remembered as complex, filled with difficulties as well as fond memories. PHR and Fortune found that, as children, nearly all of the respondents experienced economic hardships. Poverty was exacerbated by other disadvantages, for example foster care, drug use in the household, an incarcerated parent, and incomplete education. Generally living in impoverished, single-parent households, few of the respondents spoke about middle-class comforts such as family vacations, pets, arts classes or parental involvement in their schooling or health. On the other hand, not all respondents spoke negatively of their childhood and many appeared to feel great love and support in their families even under troubled circumstances.

While this research does not suggest a causal relationship between disadvantage and subsequent criminal activity, it does suggest that severe punishments meant to act as deterrents, such as the New York Rockefeller drug laws, may not succeed in preventing criminal activity. Deterrence-based sentencing assumes that a potential offender has the wherewithal to analytically assess the costs and benefits of law-abiding and criminal behavior and act on this analysis. These narratives, however, illustrate that such analytic remove would be nearly impossible for those involved in low-level drug offenses. Those struggling to "feed a habit" rarely engage in such preventive analysis. In addition, due to the relative economic deprivation and barriers faced by the people most likely to be caught up in drug crime prosecutions, there is often little perception of legitimate and realistic financial alternatives to drug involvement and involvement in drug-related crime. In light of the relative deprivation of the people most likely to be caught up in drug crime prosecution, if the Rockefeller drug

---

[59] E.g. Sheldon Danziger, Gary Sandefur & Daniel Weinberg, eds. *Confronting Poverty: Prescriptions for Change*. New York: Russell Sage Foundation. 1994.

[60] E.g. William Julius Wilson. *The Truly Disadvantaged: The Inner City, the Underclass and Public Policy*. Chicago: University of Chicago Press. 1987. Vera Institute of Justice. *The Unintended Consequences of Incarceration: Papers from a Conference*. New York: Vera Institute of Justice. 1996.

laws were intended to have a deterrent effect, it is small wonder that they have failed.

Findings from the interviews indicate that those incarcerated for drug crimes are themselves drug users, whose lives began to suffer in terms of school attendance, vocational development, and family relations due to drugs. Regardless of family circumstances, 90 percent of the respondents failed to complete high school, a problem frequently connected with drug use. Over half the respondents began using drugs while minors, several under ten years of age. Overwhelmingly, respondents told PHR and Fortune that they began their involvement with drugs through social connections including those with older siblings. For some participants, drug selling preceded drug use, for others it was the reverse. Nearly all of the respondents said that they had used drugs uncontrollably at some point and most said that they began using drugs before the age of twenty.

In spite of considerable disadvantage, most respondents said that they were optimistic about their futures particularly in their efforts to attain some degree of wealth. Yet the experiences described by respondents offer little on which to base such optimism. In most cases respondents come from unstable families and a dearth of social or educational support. For many people participating in this study, crime and drug use were ready alternatives to low wages and daily hardships.

Childhood Experiences

Family Life

Consistent with prior research,[61] the interviews yielded a pattern of disadvantage from early childhood that remained consistent throughout respondents' lives.

DS, a 47-year-old African-American woman, is typical of the respondents who spoke warmly of their childhood. She came from a "huge" family of thirteen children. Her mother was a single parent: *"My mother and I had a beautiful relationship. She tried to steer me."*

More common, though, were stories revealing complicated, difficult circumstances, and the efforts made by respondents and family members to adjust. For example, a 23-year-old African-American man, TG, grew up with an extended family made up of his mother, grandmother, aunts, uncles and cousins. He stated that his father died of liver problems associated with alcoholism, his sister was "wild" and his grandmother died in his arms when he was eight years old. He connected events from his childhood with his turn towards delinquency as a teenager:

---

[61] For example, The Correctional Association of New York. *Do They Belong in Prison? The Impact of New York's Mandatory Sentencing Laws on the Administration of Justice.* New York: The Correction Association of New York. 1985. Steven Belenko. *Behind Bars: Substance Abuse and America's Prison Population.* New York: CASA, 1998.

I stole a dollar from my grandma's dresser...the next week she died.... I was lost. I never saw anything like that before.... I felt empty. I didn't know where to go... I felt like it was my fault she died.... My family just split. Some cousins moved south. My uncle got depressed. Coked out and committed suicide.... My mother tried to help but a woman can't teach a man how to be a man.

I went to the street looking for something to heal the emptiness I felt.... I was rebellious. I got expelled from school, got into fights, was stealing. I smoked my first cigarette and first joint when I was 13 [with] my good friend.... We were up on the roof trying to stay warm.... Every nerve in my body came alive. We started laughing.

He described how he internalized the consumer culture around him and how his desire for money for himself and his family affected his behavior:

I learned the drug game by watching people.... I saw everybody with new sneakers. Saw them all with mountain bikes. I didn't want to wear 'Olympians' anymore. I hated Olympians. One day when I was playing basketball the sole fell off my shoe. I was so embarrassed, I said 'never again'. So I started selling crack. I left some money around for my mother to pay her back for the money I stole from her. ..I wanted sneakers, fast cars, money in my pocket.

Foster Care

Fourteen percent of the respondents revealed that they spent a period of their childhood in foster care.[62] An older man, JR, explained his extensive time in foster care and mental institutions from the age of five this way: "*I believe that my mother didn't want to deal with me.*" JR had four siblings all of whom were placed in foster care and from whom he was separated throughout his childhood.

In some instances, respondents reported abuse as foster children. One 26 year-old Haitian-American man, HM, described being beaten by his mother before she sent him, but not his four sisters, to foster care, where he was further abused by some foster parents:

As a boy I spent a lot of time in foster homes, group homes and DFY [Division for Youth] since coming here [the United States] in 1983. I'm told that's when I came here, I don't know...One lady beat me up when I was eleven and kept me in the basement. Locked me in the basement without any food after she beat me. I burned her house down.

---

[62] This number may be higher; respondents were not specifically asked this question in the survey.

But this same respondent, who was sent to a group home after committing arson, also spoke of his continued relationship with another foster mother who took care of him when he was six, who later visited him in prison, and about whom he wrote poetry.

Family History of Drug Use and Addiction

Over a quarter of the respondents spoke of a family history of drug or alcohol problems when describing their childhoods.[63] Drug use on the part of parents usually proved to be very disruptive. For example, JJ, a 27-year-old African-American man, described the effects of his mother's drug addiction succinctly: "My mother was on crack. She was never home, there was no food in the house, the house was in shambles. We argued. She neglected us." He himself began selling crack at 14 years of age.

Another, NV, a 29-year-old Latino man, described life in the Bronx raised as the youngest of six boys by a single mother. He last saw his father when he was 10 years old, in Sing Sing, a maximum security prison, where his father was an inmate. His father died of AIDS in 1987, having contracted it through intravenous drug use. NV said, *"My mother was a great mother, having to play both roles."* However, *"We all did our own thing. I never spent time at home. I'd disappear for two weeks at a time, then show up for a while. My brothers sold drugs – marijuana – in the streets."*

MR, a 40-year-old African-American woman grew up with her grandmother because of her parents' drug problems: *"My dad and mom separated. He was getting high. My mother did 15 years straight through in prison for robbery, for her addiction. My mother went to prison very young."* She described her grandmother as "brutally strict." She eventually went to live with her mother who, upon release from prison, was still a drug addict but who sought help, got herself off of drugs, and eventually earned a degree and found work as a social worker.

By then, MR had a drug problem of her own. Her crack addiction would have terrible consequences on her own daughter. When her daughter was 7 or 8 years old, she "was raped due to my addiction" by men who were at their home because of drugs. *"Once she was raped, I gave her to my first cousin. I can't even tell you how my daughter looks. I haven't seen her in about 11 years."*

Experiences with Juvenile Justice System

Like just over 20 percent of the sample, TG, the 23-year-old whose childhood is described above, first came into contact with the criminal justice system through its juvenile division. Between the ages of 13 and 18 he was held for a total of about two years in three juvenile facilities, Spofford, St. Cabrini, and Boys Town.

---

[63] This percentage may be higher; respondents were not specifically asked this question in the survey.

HM, whose traumatic experience with foster care is described above, was eventually removed from foster care into a Division for Youth (DFY) detention facility, was told by DFY counselors, *'we're just preparing you for the big house.' That's what where they said we were all headed.'"* Unfortunately, as the counselors predicted, *"I had friends from DFY. We went together from DFY to Comstock [Great Meadow Correctional Facility, a maximum security prison] to Washington [a medium security prison]."* For HM and for others, their experiences with the juvenile justice system served as a funnel into adult incarceration.

School

Only ten percent of people interviewed graduated high school though others later received a graduate equivalency degree (GED). School was prominent for many until an incident or their lifestyle disrupted attendance as it did for NV, who remembered: *"I got jumped once when I was going to school. It was for a pair of Patrick Ewing sneakers. They hit me with a pipe on the back of the head. I stopped going to school after that."*

Others described problems in school resulting from problems at home, like AD whose mother died when he was a child, leaving him in his sisters' care. When he decided to stop going to school in eighth grade, his sisters told him to move out of the house, and he lived on the street.

Most frequently, juvenile drug use and sales were directly associated with respondents dropping out of school. For example, LW, a 34- year-old African American man, grew up on Long Island with his mother and sister. His father died of a heroin overdose when he was one year old. He said that his family's strict rules made him rebellious. *"When I was 13 or 14, I started turning to the street, smoking and selling marijuana. I started separating from my family. When I was 16, I started selling crack and then using."* LW started skipping school and then said he was "kicked out because of poor attendance."

Juvenile Drug Use and Trade

Over half of the respondents mentioned drug use or sales as juveniles (and eighteen of these respondents mentioned using drugs other than marijuana as children). Many respondents describe a chain of events during their teenage years from private, law-abiding behavior to more social, street-based and law-breaking behavior. Nearly all of the respondents had begun using illegal drugs while still teenagers, though respondents varied in the extent of drug use and the extent to which it consumed their focus. Most of the respondents spoke about the financial benefit of selling drugs while few remembered worrying about arrest. At the same time, many who began selling for financial reasons describe instantly liking the drug they went on to use, typically heroin or crack.

One respondent described his entry to drug use from marijuana to other drugs: *"I started out with marijuana when I was twelve. [A fellow gang member] said 'go ahead, it'll make you feel good'...By the time I was thirteen, I was free-basing...I did a few pills, speed, crank, monster."*

Some began by selling for purely economic reasons and then started using drugs. One woman, EK, described her entry into drug use and sales in her early teens as economic: *"I was tired of taking care of my brother and sisters. Since my mother was a single parent all the time, I took the initiative to do things on my own. I've been on my own since I was thirteen. As soon as I left the house I was selling drugs...I learned just from watching."* Within a year she was smoking marijuana and then sniffing cocaine.

One respondent, HG, a 41-year-old man whose "whole family" was deeply involved in the drug trade in Spanish Harlem, began his involvement in the drug trade at an earlier age than most respondents. When he was 9 years old, an uncle "gave me drugs to sell to keep me from stealing." He first tried heroin at 9 years of age and then again when he was 14 or 15 years old.

Influences of Social Networks

Respondents described close involvement with friends through sports, school, dating and community activities. While these relationships were frequently brought up in describing the initiation of drug use or other delinquent behavior such as truancy and criminal activity, many respondents also referred to strong bonds between friends, girlfriends, and boyfriends. Unlike simplistic messages of negative peer pressure often cited as contributing to delinquency, most respondents portrayed some friendships and romances as critical supports, others as contributing to exposure to illegal activity, and some as competitive partnerships.

In some instances, friends benefited from the respondent's illegal activity but did not commit offenses themselves. For example RL, a 38 year-old African-American man who eventually served eight years for drug possession and a parole violation, spoke about his start in the drug trade when he was 18 years old, using money from his drug sales to buy shoes, sneakers and clothing for himself, his family and his friends. They knew where he was getting the money but were not themselves involved in the drug trade.

For others the drug trade was a part of daily life with friends and family, as it was during the childhood of HG, mentioned above, whose "whole family sold drugs" even though neither of his parents used the drugs they sold:

Everybody [the children] tried [drugs] at some time or other. I was a straight A student. But I learned to pick locks... My mother and father didn't want me selling drugs... [but] I branched out on my own and worked with my parents' connections. I wasn't worried about them telling my parents because my father would have killed them... he would have moved heaven and earth for us to go to school.

Another respondent, a 41-year-old Latino man, FZ, noted the same failure of strict parenting. Although he said that his father would hit him with a belt if he "misbehaved," he added: "*I started because...I was hanging out with a friend [whose] father sold coke. So we sold for him. I started there and moved on to heroin. I shot up heroin and coke. It was an addiction.*"

Respondents also noted the law-abiding community-based activities that provided some of their most enthusiastic recollections. These passions, whether athletic, artistic or social, existed for both those who spoke of relative happiness as a child and those who seemed to have no other happiness. For example HM, who shuttled between foster homes and juvenile facilities, also wrote poetry that he used to develop his own rap: "*I worked on mastering my flow and I got better and better. From the time I was 12 to 16...when I was home for a visit I was rapping and my uncle said,' my my, do we have a star in our midst here?'*" His uncle arranged for him to record a demo for which he received an advance payment, but when he returned to the juvenile facility he got into a fight and was prohibited from further visits home. "*My mother had to give the advance money back.*"

Sports were a part of many respondents' lives. NV, whose family experiences are described above, talked about playing "*sports with kids in the neighborhood. We used to play football at the park, even in the snow,*" he reminisced, smiling.

Adult Life before Prison

Family Life

Respondents described their adult relationships with parents, siblings, other family members, partners and children. The adult lives of many respondents often reflected the impatience and dismay of family members who tried to cope with a respondent's drug use and criminal activity. For example, LN, a 36-year-old woman and mother of two, used crack and engaged in sex for money for years both before and after her children were born. She and her husband eventually divorced, but remained in contact and he continued to try to help her and help her relationship with their children. Despite his efforts, however, she said: "*They knew I was their mother. But I wasn't their mother. They probably knew the picture of me better than they knew me.*" LN's husband eventually did not let her stay in their home, but let her come in when the children were asleep so that she could look at them. She was in and out of Rikers Island jail and eventually served a three-year sentence in three (medium and maximum security) state prisons for drug possession.

Another respondent, EK, a 40-year-old woman and mother of four, was typical in that she wished to maintain contact with her children but was also unable to care for them: *"My mom came down and got the kids. She didn't want them down there knowing that I was dealing drugs."* While EK said she saw no change in her relationship with her children, she acknowledged that she saw them "every other day and weekends" and her sisters babysat often, the two oldest children left home as teenagers and had "already had boyfriends and babies of their own" by the time she served five years in 1996 for two Class D drug sales.

The families that respondents created with partners varied in their cohesiveness. Some describe long-term committed relationships in which their partner was also their best friend. Interestingly, these relationships occurred both when the partner also used drugs and engaged in criminal activity and when the partner did not. Rarely, however did these relationships last through prison sentences to the present. Particularly for respondents who had children, it appeared that their adult families were strained often to the point of losing contact. In some cases, the other parent maintained custody of the children. In many other cases the children lived with another family member or in foster care. In several instances respondents mentioned that their children were themselves drug users or incarcerated. In spite of these challenges, many respondents spoke of repeated and tentatively successful efforts to restore relations and credibility with their children.

Legal and Illegal Employment

Few people interviewed by PHR and Fortune had stable jobs prior to state incarceration. For many this appeared to be related to ongoing drug use, severe housing instability and brief periods of incarceration in jail. Many who said they had not graduated high school were unlikely to find satisfying employment that could compare with the sums they could make selling drugs.

The amount of money available through even street-level drug sales or the support work (such as weighing and bagging drugs) that are part of the drug trade was sizable enough that even those respondents who worked full-time in legal jobs noted that they participated in the drug trade as well. In a cycle of drug use and drug-related crime, most respondents who told PHR and Fortune that they sold drugs also noted that they spent the money they earned almost immediately, mostly on drugs but also on clothing and other material goods.

For the most part, respondents described illegal work as their primary income, generally a mixture of theft and drug sales for the men and prostitution and drug sales for the women. LN, whose husband tried to be supportive, worked as stripper, an escort and prostitute, reported that she earned around $5,000 each month and spent it smoking crack.

One man, SD, was typical of the perception among respondents that the drug trade was the most obvious and lucrative employment option he saw. He described his reason for selling as self-evident: *"Everybody on my block sold drugs practically."* Another man, JM, who made minimum wage as a painter said: *"That was the reason for slingin', there wasn't enough money."*

However several respondents also spoke about legal work in their pre-prison lives, such as MN, who began working in a friend's rug restoration business while he was in college and continued this work even when he began holding large quantities of drugs in his apartment. Another man, RP, described his early legitimate work (as a driving instructor) ending because of his evident drug use. Similarly, a woman, DS, said that she had initially been opposed to her husbands' drug use while she had a steady job, and they separated because of it, but her new boyfriend "turned me on" to crack and she subsequently lost her job.

Many respondents spoke about desiring and maintaining lifestyles of considerable expense. JM, above, who was unsatisfied with a minimum wage job described how his uncle "gave[him] a brand new jeep." His uncles said: *'You don't need anything. [If] you need anything, I get it.'* Similarly, another respondent, JP, said of his spending: *"It's a keepin- up-with-the-Joneses kind of thing when you do drugs."*

Another man, AL, described the power of the financial incentive to sell drugs: *"Greed always kicks in. I doubled or tripled my income. I got a lot of material things. I could take trips… Then I started using what I was selling."* This man's family and girlfriend did not know about his drug use until the girlfriend caught him with another woman and left him. He says: *"My girl had a job. I was going to school. We had a real deep intimacy… I tried to make amends but it didn't really work. It's what drove me to be using my own stuff. When you get no forgiveness, you get in a depressed mode."*

V. PRISON EXPERIENCES

> *"When I went back to prison it felt like coming home. More than when I actually went home."*
>
> — HG, 41 years old, served five prison terms
> (four drug sales, one for manslaughter) between 1978-2002

Most respondents had multiple felony convictions – with the average being three convictions. Slightly less than a third of the group said they had only a single conviction. Additionally, nearly all respondents told PHR and Fortune that they had served short terms in the city jail system. Several people also noted that they had returned to state prison, not for new arrests but for parole violations, most of which were drug or alcohol related. While a few people spoke about the importance of interrupting their drug-using lifestyle, overwhelmingly respondents said they did not see how they benefited from their time in prison.

For most respondents, prison terms were a few years long – typically between two and four years. However, several people interviewed for this research had served much longer. Seven respondents served five to eight year terms for drug charges, and one client reported serving eleven years of a fifteen- year sentence before his sentence was commuted by Governor Pataki. In addition, because the majority of respondents had served multiple felony offenses, despite sentences on the short end of the range, some had served most of their adult lives in prison. For example, HG, a 41-year-old man, served five prison terms between the ages of seventeen and forty for a total of more than fifteen years.

The "revolving door" effect of the Rockefeller drug laws could be seen in different generations. One of the younger respondents, TG, a 23-year-old man, had already served two prison sentences (totaling about four years) after years in juvenile facilities. One of the older respondents, BA, a 54-year-old man, was sent to prison multiple times for drug sales which totaled some twenty years after his original conviction for assault of a classmate when he was sixteen (for which he received three years in an adult prison).

Most had spent time in jail prior to going to state prison and had been there more than once. However, incarceration in an upstate prison was described as more disorienting, more isolating and more brutalizing than jail terms. Consistent with literature on prison conditions, inmates reported that prisons ranged in their environments from tolerable to miserable. Most people described the prison environment as frightening, dangerous, corrupt and alienating. Uniformly, respondents cited violence among inmates and generally between correctional officers and inmates. Coping mechanisms ranged from avoidance, thus heightening isolation, to proving one's prowess through fights. Many respondents spoke about their experiences in solitary confinement, though here too, people varied in their approach to the punishment, some preferring the quiet, others saying they felt degraded and afraid. Many respondents said that they witnessed abuse from correctional officers, though most said they were not victims of such abuse. These abuses varied by facility and by individual guard but included harassment of visitors, racial slurs, insults and taunts, physical hitting and kicking, theft and sexual abuse.

Respondents also discussed the ways in which prison time affected ongoing elements of their lives, such as family relations, health issues, and an interest in abiding by the law. This research suggests the futility of using severe incarceration to combat lawlessness because almost all respondents noted that prison forced them to close up emotionally from their families, from the other people who formed their temporary community – the inmates and guards – and from themselves and their own wellbeing. Many interviewed by PHR and Fortune said that drugs were available, some going so far as to say that in prison, anything is available.

Arrest and Conviction

For many respondents their arrests and convictions for felony offenses followed years of instability. For example, LW, a 34-year-old African -American man, described how his crack use and sales from the age of 16 led to his dropping out of school and serving several short jail terms before he was sent to state prison: *"I was in and out of jail for petty larceny for shoplifting and for marijuana sale and possession and for a stolen car."* At 22, he was sent to prison following an arrest for selling crack, pled to a two to four year sentence and was not offered a drug treatment program. Several respondents linked their decision to plea bargain (96 percent of the sample pled down their last conviction) directly to the threat of the lengthy mandatory minimums under the Rockefeller drug laws. For example, FH, a 44-year-old African-American man, was caught in a drug sweep with cocaine on his person. He pled to a two to four year sentence for a drug sale despite his initial wish to go to trial in order to argue for a possession charge, not intent to sell, as he claimed that the drugs found on his person were for himself. But his lawyer told him that going to trial risked a conviction of fifteen years given that he had a prior felony sale on his record, so *"I couldn't take a chance and blow it and get fifteen years."* He added, *"There's nothing you can do about it, especially if you got no money for a real lawyer."*

Similarly, JO, a 62-year-old Native American man and Vietnam veteran, was caught in a drug sweep in 1998 and was charged with intent to sell. He had a public defender, *"who was trying to get me to cop to a plea that I didn't want. He wouldn't return my calls."* Then the judge told JO, *"if you go to trial, I can guarantee you'll do 12.5 to 25... he scared me half to death with the football numbers."* JO found out about an alternative to incarceration program in lieu of going upstate, which he requested, but was denied. He was sentenced three to six years in prison and served three years on that charge.

Long sentences as punishment for refusing treatment are not unusual and were evidenced in several people's stories as many prosecutors feel they are being lenient by offering treatment.[64] EH, a 36- year-old man originally from Puerto Rico, explained that he started selling crack when he was 27 and started using it when he was 28. When his wife found out, she kicked him out of their home. Shortly thereafter, he sold drugs to an undercover police officer on the street, and was charged with his first felony, B-level sale and possession for which he received the heightened sentence of 4.5 to 9 years after he refused to go into a drug treatment program. He said: *"Since my wife threw me out, I told the judge to put me in jail, I needed help and I didn't have no help."* Having refused treatment in what appears to be despair, he served 7 years in state prisons.

PD, a 44-year-old African-American man, with a long-time drug habit, describes his experience with a treatment alternative that he was offered. He was arrested with vials of crack in his hotel room. PD said,

> My so-called lawyer said, 'I don't think the judge is going to go for 2-4 [years]. I think he wants to give you 4.5-9.' Now TASC [the Treatment Alternatives to Street Crime program] comes into play. The judge says, 'you had too much for 2-4.' He said I had 27 grams [0.81 ounces] of crack cocaine. I heard a prosecutors talking, who said 'let's teach him a lesson. Let's give him 4.5-9.' I heard them arguing through the door. I got real loud. The judge said, 'calm down.' I took TASC because I knew they were going to give me 4.5-9. I copped out to a nursing home, when they found out I had AIDS. My stipulation — if I broke any of the rules [at the health care facility], I'd have to do 4.5-9 years.

PD broke the conditions of his sentence to a TASC-monitored treatment program for "fighting with a kid who tried to beat me out of $10" and was returned to court and sentenced to the beginning of his 4.5 to 9

---

[64] Young et al. 1998.

years, of which he served 4.5 years in five different maximum and medium security prisons. He did not participate in any drug treatment.

Prison Environment

Concern over the effects of incarceration has been raised in research on reentry and on prison-based treatment. While many in the correctional industry including the New York State Department of Correctional Services assert that incarceration is therapeutic, numerous researchers, advocates and former inmates argue that incarceration has a negative effect on inmates and their families[65] – a finding largely supported by the interviews conducted by PHR and Fortune for this report. While New York State is not among the nation's worst prison systems,[66] respondents spoke at length about the unsafe and unhealthy conditions in which they lived while incarcerated.

PHR and Fortune interviewed people who had been in at least half of the state's 71 prisons. Respondents reported that each prison has its own culture and condition, a finding in keeping with findings from the state's prison monitoring organization.[67] Generally respondents described animosity among inmates and between corrections staff and inmates. One man, BA, summed it up this way: "*The environment was always bad because COs [corrections officers] have in their head them against us and inmates have in their head us against them.*"

Abuse by Correctional Officers

Half of the women interviewed by PHR and Fortune reported having had sex with correctional officers or an awareness of it happening between inmates and correctional officers. Women described on-going coercive relationships in which guards would bring gifts and treat leniently the inmates with whom they were sexually involved, such as LN who said: "I was f——g a CO in Albion. He would bring me cigarettes." Another respondent described the ways in which some guards regularly fondled women's bodies, including their breasts, buttocks, and genitals as part of spontaneous searches conducted in cells, in corridors or elsewhere and at any time in the prison. Under New York's penal code, even "consensual" sexual relationships between inmates and corrections officers are not considered consensual.[68]

---

[65] Vera Institute of Justice, 1996. Todd Clear, Dina Rose & Judith Ryder. "Incarceration and the Community: The Problem of Returning Offenders" *Crime and Delinquency.* 47 (3) 335-351. 2001.

[66] See for example, The American Civil Liberties Union, National Prison Project. http://www.aclu.org/Prisons/PrisonsList.cfm?c=121.

[67] *State of the Prisons: Conditions of Confinement in 25 New York Correctional Facilities.* The Prison Visiting Committee. The Correctional Association of New York. 2002.

Most respondents said they witnessed physical assaults by corrections officers on other inmates but did not experience it themselves. Several others, however, said they were assaulted by officers. In these cases, the physical effects of such incidents were generally described as less significant than the psychological impact. For example, EH, who served seven years for sale and possession of crack cocaine, said:

> I had a fight and when the officers saw my black eye they demanded to know who did it. I did not want to tell as it was a fair fight. The officers took me to a room in the box [solitary confinement]. They threw my face into a wall and then threw me to the ground where my hands were cuffed behind my back. The officers started kicking me. They were racist, they called me 'spic' and 'monkey'. I had a big lump on my head and they took me to the hospital. The officers said I tried to hurt myself and I was transferred to a unit for inmates with mental problems. I stayed a week and was released ...They put me in the same prison. Would you believe that? I was scared for my life. I couldn't sleep.

Another man, RL, a 38-year-old who was incarcerated on three separate drug-related felony offenses, recounted seeing another inmate choked to death with a night stick by a corrections officer while another held the inmate's legs. The officers thought the inmate had swallowed drugs. This incident allegedly took place in Green Haven, a maximum security prison, in the early 1990s. RL said: *"I felt like it could be me. I stayed up all night, tied a sock around the cell door so it wouldn't open."*

Several respondents noted verbal abuse or intimidation by corrections officers, particularly regarding race or ethnicity. There were repeated allegations of Ku Klux Klan activity among corrections officers. OP, a 38-year-old African-American man who was held in State Corrections Institution (SCI)-Elmira in the 1980s, said: *"They had tattoos on their arms of black babies hanging from a rope, tattoos saying KKK. They were always saying, 'nigger this and nigger that.'"* In a different prison, SCI-Washington, HM, a 26-year-old Haitian-American, recounted that he became more conscious of racism in prison: *"The white COs wore pictures of black babies with ropes around their necks...The COs from Aryan Nation wore swastikas."* And another TG, a 23-year-old African-American man: *"The Klan works the prison...Those COs want the New York City crime rate up. The more niggers up there the better."* These allegations remain vague, but respondents' perception that there is organized racism among prison

---

[68] The New York Penal Code, Section 130.05 (1996) on sex offenses states that "a person is deemed incapable of consent when he or she is (...) committed to the care and custody of the State department of correctional services or a hospital; or committed to the care and custody of a local correctional facility."

officers reinforced overall frustration about racial inequalities in a system in which most inmates are minorities and most guards are white.[69]

FH, who served three years in SCI-Green Haven, a maximum security facility for a drug sale, spoke of a subtler form of abuse,

An officer come by and mark down that you want breakfast, then they don't let you out of the cell and he comes by the next day with this little smile as if nothing's happened. And meanwhile I haven't eaten and I need to eat to take my meds so I can't take my meds for HIV.

Solitary Confinement

Several inmates spoke about taking out their anger and frustration in physical fights over small incidents. These fights inevitably led to restrictions, typically solitary confinement — "the box." NL described how guilty he felt after his girlfriend died when he was in prison: *"It affected me that I couldn't go see her, that she told me to stop [using drugs]... I'm not sure if it's her dying or other things in my past that makes me stupid...I caught an attitude, any little thing would get me. I was so frustrated... I was fighting, involved with gang stuff, ended up in the box."* Another man, BA, said: *"I was thrown in the hole naked for fighting and meals consisted of bread and water. I hated the guards, who wouldn't?"*

NV reported punishment with solitary confinement following an incident at SCI-Mohawk relating to his health status: *"I was getting cans of Ensure [a dietary supplement frequently used by AIDS patients]. One CO saw it and said, 'those AIDS people [and made a sound of disgust]' I said, 'f—- you' and I got two month in the box for that."*

Solitary confinement was generally considered worse than regular prison life because it was more isolating. However a few respondents, like RL, who cycled in and out of prison for a series of drug-related crimes, felt safer in solitary confinement. During his first incarceration, he spent a total of fourteen months in solitary confinement and noted that he felt safer regarding altercations with other inmates because a person was always alone and therefore calmer. He also said that he liked the greater privacy. At the same time, he was restricted to shorter visits from family and was not allowed telephone calls.

Similarly, another man, JR, said that he felt alone, but not awful during the two years he spent in his solitary cell. He said the cell had no window other than a small one in the solid door, which was always kept closed. He

---

[69] The New York State Department of Correctional Services has a zero-tolerance policy against racist and other discriminatory displays in the workplace and further notes that officers are generally covered, so tattoos should not be visible. However, the state was unsuccessful in its efforts to fire a correctional officer who hung a banner supporting the Ku Klux Klan outside of his home, and, according to the agency's public information office, the state has not fired an employee for similar racist display in the recent past.

showered in handcuffs once a week for six minutes and was given meals through a slot in his cell door. He was allowed an hour of exercise most days, always by himself. This man had few visitors during the eighteen years that he was incarcerated.

Most, though, did not want to talk about their experiences in solitary confinement beyond indicating that it was worse than being with other inmates.

Inmate on Inmate Violence

Inmate housing is based on several factors, most prominently health and severity level of offense. Despite being convicted of nonviolent crimes, many people interviewed served portions or all of their sentences in maximum-security facilities. Consequently, in most cases, people convicted of nonviolent drug sales or related crimes were housed with inmates convicted of violent crimes including murder and rape. FH was convicted of a drug sale in 1998 and served three years in prison, including time at Green Haven, a maximum security facility. He described the ruthlessness of the people he was incarcerated with and said of that experience, *"why was they doing that to me?"*

If a person was arrested in a case that made the local news, as was the case with a few respondents, the person could be housed in the state's most secure facilities. MN said: *"I was always kept in CMC – Central Monitor Control... with high profile murders like the Happy Land fire...the serial cop killer... I knew those guys."*

Some respondents reported that inmate on inmate abuse was part of daily prison life. Several, like SR, who was a homeless crack addict when he was arrested in 1998 for a C level felony drug sale, reported incidents of makeshift weapons used on them: *"One time a guy banged me on the head with a lock. I basically ignored it."* Given the alternative of fighting, many made the effort to stay away from confrontation.

Similarly, RH: *"watching people get killed over the god damn telephone... they hit him with a shank [a self-made knife].... You've got these little kids with slash marks all because of what? ... The penitentiary puts you in a state of confusion, of animosity, not just toward the justice system but towards one another."* RH continued: *"In Elmira, people got stabbed 5, 10, 15 times with shanks. It could've been over anything.... If you looked at somebody wrong, or the fact that you was on the phone and a guy was there waiting and didn't like it and you come out and he stabs you. I seen about 6 or 7 people get murdered, 15 or more get stabbed."*

Others described a coping mechanism of hiding how they felt. As LY described his first incarceration when he was 16 years old:

> I was frightened but I couldn't show it.... If they see you're afraid, they categorize you as a chump... take their misery out on you.... Weakness shows in how you carry yourself, how you talk, how you treat people.

Strength is… not stressing, not crying…. It's a masquerade. You hide your anger.

Another, DS, echoed this approach as she used it in a woman's prison: *"I learned to mind my own business. One girl, she was aggressive. I had to fight her, had to show I was strong. I spent 13 days in the hole [solitary confinement] for that."*

Several respondents described the especially traumatic experience of being incarcerated in adult prisons as teenagers. One, HM, who first entered an adult prison at age 16, said: *"I learned shit, it made me tougher… I learned a lot about how to survive in prison and out of prison. Like how to pull credit card scams."* HG echoed this sentiment: *"I was in and out of the box. I got into a lot of fights. As an adolescent in jail, basically you got to fight to stay alive."* Another man, TG, described the effect of his early experiences in juvenile detention facilities: *"Someone eyeballs you [you respond] most likely with fights… It made me more or less emotionless… I got hit with a lock in a sock at St. Cabrini."*

Sexual relations were another part of the abusive environment according to many of the respondents. For the most part the men interviewed said that consensual homosexual relationships existed in prison between inmates and many said they felt threatened by them. The men who had been in prisons as teenagers were particularly clear that they felt coerced into homosexual relationships, which they tried to avoid.

For example, OP, a 38-year -old African -American man, first served eighteen months in prison for a robbery relating to his drug use while a teen. He says,

> *At sixteen I was sent to Elmira maximum security. I was one of the first convicted [of robbery] under the new guidelines for prosecuting juveniles as adults [after the "adult" age was lowered in New York to 16 from 18]. It was a frightening situation, a scary experience. You hear those bells ring, those doors slam. That's what you go to sleep by and wake up by. I had no hair on my face. I was a baby, fighting for my life, hoping I could come out alive.*

OP got himself onto the boxing team in order to develop self-defense skills and to be able to protect himself from the "booty bandits" – men who "like young boys." Young men tried to stay away from them. "I did," OP said. Between the ages of 26 and 37, OP served three sentences on felony drug sale and possession charges.

Drug Availability

Incarceration had radically different impacts on respondents' drug use. While some stated that incarceration stopped their street drug use, others said drugs were widely available and that they continued to use drugs in prison.

Those respondents who said that they did not use drugs while incarcerated differed in their reasons, with the minority saying that they tried to stop using altogether and most saying that prison was simply a break from their street drug use to which they returned when released. People in this group noted that the decision not to use drugs while in prison was based largely on a desire to stay away from trouble with other inmates. Strikingly, some of those who chose not to use drugs in prison conceptualized their "clean time" as a practical decision about their own well-being, both in terms of the social costs of drug use in prison and the physical effects of drug use on their bodies. The decision not to use drugs while in prison was akin to a decision to go on a retreat, suggesting the potential for self-directed health decision-making in drug treatment.

Almost all of the respondents said that they could get illegal drugs while in jail and in prison. While not all continued to use drugs in prison, many did, like MN who continued to inject heroin, and HG who sold it. One man, TH, said he repeatedly got back into drugs no matter which prison he was moved to. After repeated fights and stints in solitary confinement, this man said he was caught using drugs: "*I was so high I couldn't even pee. I did a year in the box, lost all sorts of privileges.*" Another man, RL, like many, said he smoked marijuana regularly and occasionally sniffed cocaine. A third man, LW, said: "*I knew who was selling and using. It was like a little New York, same drugs as on the street. They were easy to get if you have the money.*" A woman, TS, said she learned skills in prison but at the same time continued to use and sell drugs which were readily available or smuggled in: "*Around the Entenmanns cake there was a bundle or two of dope up around the edges.*"

BA's drug habit actually began in prison. He first tried cocaine in the early 1980s while serving time in prison for a non drug-related offense. Upon release he began freebasing, becoming addicted. For the next sixteen years, he used and sold cocaine until his felony conviction for drug sales in the late 1990s.

One woman, MR, described the seeming irrelevance of custody for drug use: "*You always get high on Rikers, with pills, weed, heroin. Rarely do you get to smoke crack. They release me in the middle of the night and I'm high. Here I am high at 3:30 a.m. on Queens Boulevard. So what do you expect happens?*" MR was "*busted again, busted like a suitcase.*"

Drug Treatment, Educational and Vocational Programs in Prison

Program availability varies by prison. Respondents' opinions varied about the availability and utility of the drug treatment, educational and training programs in prison, but most said they were willing to try any program offered, such as MS, who said: "*I got into as many things as I could.... There were waiting lists for programs.*" Most respondents who participated in programs, whether therapeutic or educational, cited the hope that program participation could improve their chances of securing release on parole.

A major problem in prison-based programs is that the quality of many prison programs is notoriously difficult to assess and generally not examined. In addition to program dropout (either because of prison transfer or because the inmate stops attending) the content of programs varies considerably.

Drug Treatment and other Therapeutic Programs

More than half the sample had participated in drug treatment including the Comprehensive Alcohol and Substance Abuse Treatment Program (CASAT) and Alcohol and Substance Abuse Treatment (ASAT), two part-time drug education and treatment programs operated by the Department of Correctional Services. Respondents also spoke about the availability of self-help groups including Alcoholics Anonymous, Narcotics Anonymous and the HIV groups. These meetings are common in prisons in part because of their generally rehabilitative mission and the low (generally no) cost to prison administrators.

Therapeutic programming was usually the first drug treatment for people in this study, and was inconsistent in quality and availability. People interviewed for this research described being taken out of treatment when they were moved to different prisons, mediocre treatment, and a dearth of continuity in treatment – all of which are targeted as responsible for low success rates in the drug treatment literature.

For example, MN told interviewers that he was in a program for domestic violence, but when asked, he said that he had never hurt a woman and that domestic violence had never been an issue for him, but that the program also addressed addiction, so he was put in for that reason. NT, a 39-year-old man who served 2.8 years for a Class C drug possession charge, said, *"I did the CASAT program upstate. The civilian guy left, they put me in charge of CASAT and I didn't have any education or training... But I think I did pretty good."*

Many went into every program they could in a combination of need for services and boredom. For example during his three sentences and additional periods when he was returned for parole violations, TH, who was 34 years old, got his GED, entered at least three drug programs, a couple of vocational programs and at least one additional education program. His case illustrates one of the problems of prison-based programming: he described being moved from one prison to another based on security classification and prison census, regardless of program availability and participation. He was taken out of a drug program that he felt was helpful for him and then placed in a prison that had no comparable program. For these respondents, with drug treatment programs, a twelve-step drug abuse treatment program such as Alcoholics Anonymous might be followed by a faith-based program or a therapeutic community model or by nothing at all.

Other people had better experiences, such as SR, a 51-year-old African-American man who was able to enter residential drug treatment upon his release from prison thanks to his involvement in CASAT while at SCI-Marcy. One woman, YT, described attending drug addiction information classes (ASAT and CASAT), GED classes and trade classes in plumbing, cosmetics and computer skills. She said: *"[Prison] is where I learned about addiction... I learned there was help... I learned stuff for a job...I started to learn there was hope."* Several mentioned the helpfulness of anger management classes. EF recalled how when he was angry: *"I used to just react. I now know different: that it's better for me to think about the consequences before reacting."*

Beyond inconsistency in program availability, several respondents voiced frustration with the quality of prison-based treatment. CK, a 38-year-old Latino with three felony drug sales on his record, participated in the Department of Correctional Services' "Shock Incarceration" program at Lakeview for one of his convictions as well as in a CASAT program in prison, said,

> *Lakeview was tough. Different people need different time. I hadn't reached that level. It [Lakeview] is not treatment.... [And with CASAT,] the people there are mostly scared and mostly motivated by fear. Real treatment is different, its clinical such that with time and patience, you open up and build trust. But [in CASAT] you just sit in class and hear blah, blah, blah. You sit in a hard chair, some teacher talking and it just doesn't reach you. It's just them saying 'we got the program, we're spending the money.' That's a crock.*

NT, the man, above, who was made a lead instructor of a CASAT program and who completed several treatment programs while incarcerated said:

> *Usually they just herd you here and there. I didn't get anything out of the programs. I've done ASAT, CASAT, Osborne. I'm programmed out. These programs actually slow you down. It makes you frustrated.... They didn't teach me how to be sober. I did that myself.*

Educational/Vocational Programs

Several valued the educational and vocational programming available to them in prison. For example, EH said he enjoyed a computer technician course he took in prison (he was transferred before he could complete it) and said of his prison time, "I was good at fixing things and fixed things for other inmates, like radios." He said he hoped to take another computer maintenance course now that he was out of prison. Among those who said they valued vocational development in prison. However, several seemed to accumulate certifications and new skills without any apparent strategy. YT, quoted above, who greatly appreciated the programs, described a disconnected list of prison-based training: *"in prison, I almost got my GED. I learned plumbing, cosmetology, did computer lab."* LN, like some others however, believed these programs were not helping her outside of prison: *"You get these groups and stupid s——- classes you can get and little certificates you get… there's no place to go get a welding job or experience with the little bitty [prison] experience."*

Prison Experience and Impact on Health

Healthcare in Prison

Prison was the first place many respondents described receiving ongoing medical care, and it was the place where many were told about specific medical conditions, notably HIV infection. Many respondents developed symptoms of chronic disease while incarcerated including asthma, heart disease, epilepsy, ulcers and cancer. While many spoke of receiving prompt care in prison, most respondents noted differences between prisons, which was especially problematic if an inmate was transferred from prison to prison with a health condition.

For example one man, TN, said he was treated relatively well when he had his first heart attack in SCI-Attica, but that at SCI- Marcy he was kept in a drug treatment program that required too long a walk from his cell and that it took months of his complaining and several collapses in the hallway before the prison accepted that he should not be required to make the long walk. The same man reported being forced by corrections officers to eat food that was not allowed by his post-heart attack diet.

Another, NL, a 36-year-old with multiple Class C drug convictions and who was HIV positive, said that he had no complaints about healthcare at SCI-Mohawk, but SCI-Ogdensburg *"really sucked, a lot of people dying from AIDS and other complications not being taken to an outside hospital. Basically, they just leave sick people lying in their beds rather than taking them to the hospital."*

AD, a 54-year-old man, was diagnosed with Hepatitis C upon reception for his second drug conviction but was only told over a year later in a different facility. He then was transferred to a third facility where *"the doc was trying to help but the doc was denied by Albany to get a biopsy to see if I had liver damage."*

FH, a 44-year-old man, reported: *"On Rikers I had a job that they didn't give me the proper protective clothing…I was working in the kitchen and ended up with a back brace and a cane. When I was transferred to Green Haven [a maximum security prison] they took the back brace and cane to shackle me and didn't give them back."*

New York State prisons provide, but do not require, HIV testing. Testing is voluntary. Twenty respondents in the sample said they were HIV positive and of those sixteen learned their status when they were incarcerated.[70] Indeed, New York has the highest percentage of state and federal prison inmates known to be HIV positive in the country.[71] Prisoners, like the HIV-infected population in the US at large, are overrepresented by communities of color and characterized by high rates of poverty, high risk behaviors such as intravenous drug use, and poor access to preventive and primary healthcare.[72] While most of these people were tested as part of their health-care while in custody, several said they were diagnosed only after they developed an opportunistic infection (usually pneumocystis carinii pneumonia) associated with AIDS. For example, CP, a 38-year-old African-American woman, described how she learned that she was HIV positive: *"I was just draggin'. An officer looked at me and the picture on my ID and said it was not the same person. I had pneumonia. I was two weeks in the hospital. If the sergeant didn't do his job, I wouldn't be alive."*

Another respondent, SR, who learned that he was positive for both TB and HIV in prison, was appreciative of the care he received at SCI-Cape Vincent: *"I thought the health staff was great. They made sure I was there every day to take my meds."*

Mental Health

Several respondents said that prison shaped their characters in negative ways. For example, MR, a 40-year-old woman whose family history of addiction and own crack addiction is described in the previous section, said:

> *I'm not violent. But that's what [prison] made you. You actually had to become that to survive. You had to change...to put aside your values, your morals.... [Once released] I had a verbal altercation with this girl and I thought, 'she doesn't know where this is going to go. We're going into the hospital or jail if she pushes me.'*

Another person, NT, said: *"It shuts you. It makes you less emotional. You see someone getting raped, I'm sorry for you, but it's not my thing."* Some respondents, like OS, seemed to simultaneously appreciate and

---

[70] This high number may be explained by the fact that Fortune offers HIV services.

[71] Over 8 percent were estimated to be HIV positive in 2001. Bureau of Justice Statistics Bulletin. *HIV in Prisons, 2001.* US Department of Justice. January 2004.

[72] See David S. MacDougall. "HIV/AIDS behind Bars." *Journal of the International Association of Physicians in AIDS Care.* 1998;4(10): 18-24.

revile the way prison changed them: *"[Having stopped using crack and heroin in prison] I regret that I went there, the whole deal. It made me angry towards myself."*
FH stated:

> *You feel like something has reached down inside you and snatched your insides out and leaves you heartless. At [SCI-] Green Haven it's a max where 75 percent of the guys had life. You slow down and realize they've got 10-15 years more in here. It f—- you up. The abuse and nastiness that some people will have to live with, think about it and how it makes you into something I'm not.*

Many alluded to the change that took place as a consequence of solitary confinement. One man was sent to "the hole" after fighting with a corrections officer. He said:

> *Every three hours they cracked the door, you have a stream of light coming through the side of the door. You stand outside the cell three times a day for ten minutes. There's not even enough space to do push-ups. Once a week you got a shower. You had a hole to urinate and defecate in. You had toilet paper. I felt like an animal. It takes a lot to cope.*

For others solitary confinement was an alternative to the routine stress of prison life. For example, PY, a white 46-year -old man: *"The worst part of prison was being surrounded by people you don't want to be with. You don't want to bug out and go in protective custody, it's isolation. But there are many who are violent or psychologically crazy. There's no getting away."*

The prevalence of incarceration can lead some to feel that life in prison is inevitable or even preferable to life outside of prison, and that minority communities may be particularly susceptible to this delusion because of the disproportionately high percent of their members who are or have been incarcerated.[73] This problem was documented in a few of the interviews. For example, one man, JR, described his incarceration as reassuring:

> *The COs used to tell me, 'everyone wants to go home but you're the opposite. What's wrong with you? You're too institutional'...Sometimes there's so much bulls—- on the street, you know? I think it's better to lock me up and throw away the key, man, and leave me alone...To be honest, when I get so frustrated [with his life being hard and unfair], man, yes, you hit it right on the head, I feel safer locked up.*

Another man, HG, told of a similar feeling: *"When I went back to prison it felt like coming home. More than when I actually went home. I was drifting further away from my family."*

---

[73] E.g. Wacquant, 2000.

Rather than regard their experiences in prison as rehabilitative, this sample overwhelmingly worried that prison had changed them for the worse, making them more suspicious, less trusting, less caring and more angry than they remembered being before incarceration.

Prison and the Family

Many respondents said that they did not receive many visitors and lost contact with loved ones while incarcerated. The distance of upstate prisons from New York City, where the respondents were from, was frequently cited as a problem, as was their shame at being in prison or their loved ones' frustration at their often frequent incarcerations.

People like MS, a 38-year-old man with three children who served 6.5 years for two drug felony sentences, spoke about the disappointment of one of the women with whom he had been involved (and with whom he had a daughter): *"I wrote, I wrote, I wrote, and I never got anything back. I scraped together the money to send my daughter a gift at Christmas and still I never heard."*

JO, 62 years old, said, *"My daughter wanted to come see me. But I felt like I didn't want her to see me locked down like an animal."* As if speaking to his daughter, he said, *"When you come and I look in your face and the hurt and the degradation, nah, I couldn't take that s——."*

Many of the men in the sample spoke of children they never saw. JH, a 58-year-old man and addict who most recently served four years in state prison for possession of heroin, described his children's perception of him this way: *"They didn't really like me. I'm in and out of the penitentiary. I'm not there when they're born, Major events come along and I'm not there. They are tired of this jail stuff, they think, my daddy's a jailbird and they can't talk about their daddy."*

While many spoke about family and spouses severing relations after conviction, several said that they were responsible for stopping contact out of shame, disappointment and guilt. A man, TH, said: *"I wrote my wife and said, 'don't even write. I can't feel it."*

Others spoke of regular contact in spite of continued drug use and incarceration. For example RH, a 43-year-old man who served twelve years in state prisons for four offenses and parole violations said: *"Without family ties I wouldn't have gotten this far. This is very important, that you have family ties at your first downfall. They didn't reject me."* This man's family was primarily his older siblings and his three daughters. He kept in touch with them mainly through letters, *"I wouldn't drag anybody out eight hours, ten hours to come out and see me for just a few hours."* RH's family regularly sent him money [to buy goods in the prison commissary], cards and letters as well as telephone calls.

CP, a 38-year-old African-American woman with two teenage children, served a year in prison for a drug sale. While in SCI-Bedford, a maximum security prison, she maintained family contact and received visits from them on "Family Day." She recalled, *"Family Day, I loved that. We go to the vending machines and just are doing things together. One time, I cried so much that the officer gave me ten more minutes."*

Many regretted their absence with a mixture of concern, hurt pride and lingering sadness described by a respondent, CW: *"Everybody's going through some stress. You think, who's robbing your mom? Who's sleeping with your wife?"* At the same time this man was still upset about his family's rejection of him during his incarceration, he went on: *"Get rid of the family. When I needed you all, you wasn't there."*

Another man, MS, said: *"[My daughter] got on the phone and asked, 'Daddy, why you in jail?' In those two seconds I had to decide whether to tell them the truth. I've been lying for too long, I'm going to tell the truth...You know kids ask tough questions."* This man is now trying to restore that relationship: *"She is still upset, but she's seeing it's getting better. She knows she will hear from me."*

Overall, respondents reported a disturbing familiarity and resignation to the toughening effects of incarceration. While some spoke about the utility of taking a break from the street, and a few found the highly structured environment a welcome alternative to the chaos of their lives on the streets, most people interviewed found little or nothing of value in their incarceration. Many were bitter about the treatment they received and the general harshness of the prison environment. Others expressed resentment that they were incarcerated for nonviolent, petty offenses.

VI. RE-ENTRY

> *"I still have drug dreams. But I have to constantly stay in therapy. That's why I'm in treatment, so I don't go back."*
>
> – SR, 51-year-old man who was a formerly homeless crack addict and who served prison time for a felony drug sale.

In keeping with findings that are emerging from recent academic interest in prisoner re-entry to society, PHR and Fortune found that people coming out of prison faced significant and diverse difficulties that appear to eclipse the goal of remaining drug and crime free.

Seventy percent of the people interviewed for this report had attempted re-entry into society on parole before their most recent release and had been returned to custody either for a new offense or for a parole violation. While some spoke of newfound hope and will to stay out of prison, others said that upon earlier releases from prison they had also sought to repair family relationships, find legitimate employment and avoid drugs. For many who spoke of these hopes, the realities of trying to mend their lives were less clear than their intentions.

Time in prison meant further loss of family connection for most respondents. Even those who maintained contact with family noted the psychological and emotional duress of being absent for their children's birthdays, schooling and daily questions, or the death of a parent, or simply missing the daily events of their loved ones' lives. For those who did not have significant contact with family during incarceration, the divide was greater still. Respondents spoke about not knowing their children, or worse, being considered a criminal – a bad person – by their families. This physical and emotional distance from family members made return more difficult for most respondents because of the ambivalent feelings many family members continued to hold.

Personal difficulties were frequently matched by the difficulties many faced in trying to achieve and maintain financial stability. Several respondents said that they could not find jobs or were fired once a prospective employer discovered their criminal record. Others spoke about the difficulty of managing on low-wage jobs and the on-going temptation to make money in the drug trade. Many respondents described these numerous sources of stress as influencing factors in their ability to abide by parole regulations, maintain sobriety and avoid criminal activity.

Living Conditions upon Re-entry

Most respondents interviewed for this report cited numerous difficulties in maintaining their livelihood upon return from prison. These included problems with housing, ongoing health concerns, difficulty finding and keeping legal work and a reliance on public benefits that generally were not secured at the time of their release.

Housing

Most respondents lost their housing as a consequence of drug use, conviction or incarceration. Typically, a respondent's drug use or incarceration led to family reluctance to allow that person to remain in the home. At the same time, due to federal public housing laws enacted in the 1990s, much public housing is forbidden to people with a felony drug conviction even if family wants to take the ex-prisoner back.[74] Following federal provisions, New York City maintains a discretion-based policy, meaning it is up to individual public housing directors to decide who lives in a building's units. The law prohibits convicted felony offenders from residing in Section 8 and other public housing for a specified (and varying based on offense) period of time after conviction. Thus even those families that wish to maintain ties can be placed in a position of having to deny their relative a home.

Further, people on parole are prohibited from contact with other parolees, so families and friends who are on parole cannot live together. Between these personal and systemic barriers to stable housing, many respondents said that they moved around upon release from prison and had yet to establish stable housing.

Of the fifty people interviewed, eighteen had been or were homeless after release from prison, and fifteen were living in temporary social service residences. Nearly all the others described moving between parents, partners, other family members and friends after release.

One man's experience, JO, a 62-year-old Vietnam veteran, was typical. He lost his apartment when he was incarcerated and was released to a shelter, which he left almost immediately because: *"the shelter was terrible. Nobody's working; there's people using drugs; everybody's taking stuff from you."* He moved to a single-room occupancy hotel, then to a

---

[74] For an overview of federal restrictions see, *Housing Laws Affecting Individuals with Criminal Convictions* New York: The Legal Action Center. 2000. See http://www.lac.org/pubs/gratis/housing_laws.pdf and *Public Housing Laws Affecting Individuals with Criminal Records in New York City*. New York: The Legal Action Center. 2001. See http://www.lac.org/modules/ncjta/nyc.pdf.

YMCA, then to a room he rented from a person he met in AA. At the time of the interview, he was living with a girlfriend in another rented room.

Concern about safety and drug use in the shelters was a common theme. One woman, MR, whose family history of addiction and whose crack addiction was detailed in previous sections, saw extensive drug use by residents in the Jamaica, Queens shelter to which she was released from prison. A man, CK, said of the shelter on Ward's Island: *"People were smoking crack. I was smelling it. It was disgusting."* Another described his experience at the same shelter: *"It was not a good place for me. I smell weed and seen drugs and I trying to stay off that. They're off the hook there. People are doing crazy stuff."* A woman, KH, said that in order to avoid fights in the shelters (and the involvement of the police) she would bring all of her belongings with her wherever she went, including into the shower, so that no one would try to take them.

Respondents who lived with their friends or families reported varied environments. For some drugs remained an ongoing problem in the home because of friends' or family members' drug use. For example one woman, AM, described leaving a shelter because of drug use, only to start using drugs with the friend she went to stay with.

One woman, TS, who cycled in and out of jail, prison, residential treatment, SROs (single room occupancy housing) and friends' apartments said:

"When I was released I stayed clean for two and a half months, then I was arrested and went to Rikers [Island]. I was trying to get into a program while I was on Rikers and I lost my apartment in the projects. It was devastating. I was in [a residential program] for a year, then I moved to an SRO [where the location] kicked up my shit again because I could look out my window and see people selling... Now I am in another SRO where I do security and maintenance work."

Attitudes and Expectations toward Rehabilitation

In order to avoid returning to prison, most respondents offered common maxims of treatment, such as avoiding "people, places and things" and, even more broadly, "staying out of trouble." People like LY offered modest efforts at life change: *"My plan is to stay out of jail...Take a life sciences class."*

However, many who PHR and Fortune interviewed expressed strong optimism about their futures, typically citing their last prison experience as somehow different from others. But this optimism sometimes seemed misplaced given past failures at rehabilitation upon release from prison and at times unrealistic-sounding expectations for the future.

For example, one respondent, FZ, a 41-year-old man who served four prison sentences for drug sales over the last 15 years, said: *"On my last bid I started challenging myself... I have perseverance. I'm going to do it... I got to be more dedicated to people's needs. I'm hurting myself and other people... I realized I'm not that stupid after all."* But this same man also was unemployed, was staying illegally in a friend's public housing apartment and voiced confusion and worry about his situation generally:

The more you bring me down, the stronger I'll be...People say I'm no good. I've got no friends. I don't get close to people. I'm afraid. I'm trying to get a job...I want to go back to school. I don't think I can get a job in the trades I learned in prison. Maybe I could get a plumbing and heating license, maybe buy a computer.

His search for the way to stay out of prison did not seem aided by numerous vocational certifications he received during his time in prison.

Some participants cited family as a critical compliment to any program. For example, DS said *"I didn't want to lose my family. And I was tired of druggin."* Some also had established routines that they felt confident would sustain them. For example, CP, a 38 -year-old HIV-positive woman had a job and an apartment:

I'm working as a health aide... But I can't give them their medicines. I make $250 a month... I get food stamps.... Now I'm living in the Bronx in an apartment that's paid for by DAS [NYC Division of AIDS Services]. There's not much money. I have to pay Con Ed and get a Metro card every month. In March I have a court date to get back my kids. My boyfriend's kids stay with me sometimes... My brothers, they all can't believe it that I'm all set up on my own.

Others expressed worry about their coping mechanisms after incarceration, namely the short fuses they developed in prison. JO said that he had to change his outlook because *"I would have hurt somebody. I came home with an attitude... everybody's the enemy... When in the subway, somebody's steppin' on my shoes and I say you get off my shoes."* LN said, *"I didn't know who I was when I came out. People in prison are very tough and I showed them you can't f—- with me. People aren't that way outside. People are lookin' at me like 'you're crazy.'"*

Overall, given the multiple drug convictions of this sample, the negative experiences in prison rarely appeared to result in people changing their lifestyles to such a degree that they did not at some point return to prison, either for a violation of parole or another offense, frequently the same type of drug offense that they had been convicted of before. For example, YT said, *"The first bid had the most effect on me. It's when I learned the most and when it was roughest for me."* Yet this same woman continued to use drugs (adding heroin to her crack use) and cycle in and out of jail and prison.

Employment

Most of the persons interviewed did not have stable or full-time employment at the time of the interview. While many people described skills they had and training programs in which they participated, many said that the vocational programs were not helpful in getting a job on the outside, and almost everyone said that their criminal record impeded their job search. *"It's really, really difficult getting employment when you've been in prison,"* said TG, a 23-year-old man who served time in juvenile facilities and served time in state prison for a drug sale. He did not know how to account for this time on his resumé.

Not surprisingly given that the sample was drawn from a direct service organization, respondents reported high levels of activity in job training, educational programming and other services. Many seemed willing to enter any program they could get in to. These activities were not linked with training in prison and frequently respondents' career plans appeared to have no connection to prior efforts. For example, CS, 48-year-old man who served two short terms in prison for cocaine possession, reported that he worked as a messenger, dress cutter, and had performed some clerical work prior to prison. In prison, he learned how to clean walls and carpets and how to strip floors. He said he had recently become motivated to get his GED and that he hoped to become a radiology technician at a hospital where a friend was chief of radiology. AL, who had already worked as a carpenter took maintenance and carpentry vocational training in prison, which he valued. But the same man now said he wanted to *"learn computers and develop a career in it...I also want to mix music. I like the gospel groove...I'd like to start a business with my uncle."*

In addition, many of the respondents had not changed their interest in making as much money as quickly as possible, but were now willing to do so through legitimate employment. These aspirations often seemed disconnected from the realities of the person's situation. One 27-year-old man described his aspirations this way: *"I could do anything [with a commercial driver's license], drive a bus, a truck. After I get my CDL [commercial driver's license] I want to find out about crane operators. Hopefully when I am 38 or 39 I won't have to work anymore. Maybe I can have a house. I don't want to work for too long. I want to be retired."* Similarly, JM, who was experiencing difficulties keeping a job, said: *"I want to own a hotel or a restaurant. I manage money real well."*

Many respondents, however, expressed the wish to work as a peer counselor, using either their HIV or drug experience to help others. For example, KH, an HIV-positive woman, who had been addicted to heroin and crack, served a 2.5 year prison sentence for possession. She said that she hoped to be trained in HIV and drug education and then find work in those areas.

Frequently respondents described difficulties in maintaining jobs when they found them. For example, a man, JM, who had held several jobs and said he hoped to join a union, described working 13-hour shifts with no lunch hour cooking at a popular casual dining chain restaurant: *"when I complained, I lost my job."*

Frustrated about being unable to make money, several respondents, like CP, noted the risk that if they didn't work they would eventually go back to using drugs: *"When I got home I couldn't sleep and my mind would say 'you can go out.' I struggled with that. My mom would say 'why you clean the house every day?' I got to stay active."*

Several people also implied that the emotional changes they went through to survive in prison were detriments in job interviews. For example, NT: *"I'm more cynical. Everybody's got a hustle or an angle on you...It can make it harder to make friends. You might show it without realizing it and it can hurt you getting a job."*

Reconnecting: Family and Social Networks

Family

Some respondents reported that the critical support of family throughout incarceration continued to buoy them once they came home, but more commonly the former prisoners interviewed for this study described ongoing mistrust and frequently anger from family. Often even supportive family members and spouses were wary of whether the respondent would go back to using drugs and prison. Several of the respondents indicated that such doubt was well placed as they had returned to jail or prison several times, either for parole violation or for new drug offenses.

Overwhelmingly, respondents describe the importance of restoring their relationships with family members, including parents, siblings, partners and children. Respondents described these relationships, when they were positive, as enormously rewarding. For example, a 38-year-old man, RL, who was incarcerated on four separate drug-related offenses, described his relationship with his parents: *"I talk with them every day. I am very close with my dad now. We joke around, sit and watch football. I don't know how to express it. I told my father I love him."*

From the interviews, relations between respondents and their children appeared both especially fragile and especially important. For example, one 46-year-old woman, KH, said she rarely saw her six children while she was using drugs but said that she now has great relationships with her children and grandchildren, and that her children regularly try to convince her to move closer to them. KH said that she was nervous at first about explaining her long absences to her children, but that they were supportive. Indeed, she reported that she still feels like getting high sometimes, but does not because she knows her children would be so against it. Her drug use and prison time left her three sons and three daughters living with other family members. One of her sons ran away several times and is now incarcerated. Her new relationships with her children were bittersweet: one daughter, when speaking of her childhood, has asked her from time to time, *"why didn't you come get me?"*

Likewise, for others, like RP, family was both supportive and challenging because of the apparent ease with which family members had achieved some measures of success. He said:

> *Growing up I was tight with my cousin. I was supposed to be the one who would succeed. We used and partied together, but it wasn't heavy addiction back then. My cousin got out of the city, found a good woman and got a good job...he has a house and five kids...It makes me feel bad about myself. I had the same opportunity and didn't take advantage of it.*

For others the transition back to regular family relations was not possible. JO said: *"Prison broke up a good relationship with my wife. I wasn't there to give her support... It left me with the feeling that I didn't care what happened to me."* Another man, JH, who had not seen his daughter in years, put it: *"They are still mad at me."* A 30-year-old woman, YT, woman who was addicted to crack and served time for a series of drug charges, said she has no contact now with three of her five children, *"their grandmother's hiding them from me"* and she is trying to obtain a court order for visitation rights. She had successfully sought visitation with her fourth child and is the sole custodial parent of her fifth child, a two-month old baby, whom she said has kept her going and has changed her attitude towards drugs and has made her want to stay abstinent and out of prison.

Social Networks

Friends and acquaintances play a mixed role in the lives of most of the people interviewed for this report. In drug abuse treatment many respondents were warned that their drug use was related to their social circles. At the same time, respondents described the loneliness and internalized stigma of criminal activity and incarceration as oppressive and stressful, suggesting that the isolation of cutting off social ties could also lead to relapse to drug use. Respondents described on-going efforts to differentiate between positive and negative social relationships, and additional efforts to restore and strengthen the former, while avoiding the latter. Again and again, respondents offered examples of the difficulty of this calculation.

YT described conflict-laden relationships with her family including no contact with three of her five children. She thought that the lack of contact with her family led to her efforts to socialize.

When I first got out after work release, I was living in the living room in the house of a father of a friend, a friend who got killed as a result of life on the streets…But then I went back to people, places and things. Loneliness was part of it. I said to myself, let me go check out some friends and it started again. This friend's father had tried to help and tried to take me off the streets. He was mad at me going back to drugs.

Several people spoke about the difficulty of overcoming the suspicions they developed in prison. One man, TN, stated: *"The violence [in prison] bred fear. The fear made me not have trust in people. Nowadays, not only when I see drug activity, but if there is a crowd at all, I walk over to the other side of the street."*

Many tried to stay away from old friends associated with their preprison life. For example, TH: *"I'm in the same neighborhood. When I see guys these guys [persons involved with drugs]…I keep movin.' I ain't got time for that."*

Drug Use and Trade

The respondents' experiences demonstrate the difficulty of maintaining sobriety and/or avoiding the drug trade given unsuccessful treatment interventions and economic and social incentives to use and trade. Frequently, the pattern of resolve to avoid drugs followed by succumbing to the prevalence of drugs in the community proved too difficult to overcome.

Indeed, many respondents reported continuing drug use and sales. For example, 23-year- old TG described his return to drugs as a natural inclination to what he knew how to do: *"It's hard when you get out of prison. A lot of us have to rely on the hook- up. After the [halfway house], I sold marijuana a little to make ends meet."*

In addition, many people relapsed because they underestimated the challenges to remaining drug free and did not always conceptualize a one-time decision to use drugs or alcohol as a slippery slope. One man, RP, described his relapse this way: *"I thought I deserved to have a beer and it's like: pow, you are back in the addiction. I was gradually pulling away from my support system…I don't think I 'm scared of success; it's more like I forget where I came from."* While the reference to support is a basic tenet of 12-step recovery programs, this man also describes his own optimistic assumption that he could casually use drugs without returning to out-of-control addiction.

Several respondents seemed resigned to their addiction, but had established harm-reduction routines, such as JR who used methadone and was certain he would return to heroin without it. Another man, JH, who was homeless, seemed resigned to a life of drug use and incarceration: "*I take dope now and then to feel better. When I go to [Rikers] island, it's detox.*" The same man then noticed his apparent hopelessness: "*I'm a little embarrassed. Here I am about 60 and I ain't got nothing.*"

Others continue to use drugs but insisted that they were able to do so without regular use. MN said that he used cocaine about once each month and that he did not want to stop because he enjoyed it. He also said that he lived with his wife, who was using drugs regularly, but was also working full-time to support them both. Another man, JH, saw little reason to stop using and had become quite accustomed to the legal consequences of his drug use: "*I take dope now and then to feel better. When I go to the Island [jail] I go to detox.*" Still others said that their involvement with drugs was only to help friends, for example, SH, who was arrested in November 2002 when, he said, he bought drugs for a friend who was a user. He was awaiting his next court appearance to see whether the B-level felony might be reduced so that he could avoid a return to state prison.

Still others had a holistic view of recovery, such as one man, RH, who had been abstinent for five years:

> I was just tired. I said I can't do the things I want to, help with my kids…All the programming in the world is not going to help if a person don't want to change…The motivation has to come from within. But the programming, the information, the structure, counselors, it all helps get people to the place where they want to change.

Parole Supervision

Everyone interviewed was or had been under parole supervision, a system intended to provide oversight and support as a means of prisoner reentry. In reality, parole caseloads are notoriously large, and parole officers have little in the way of training or guidelines to help them do their work. Consequently, many focus their efforts on parolee supervision. Relationships with parole officers, even within one individual respondent's experiences, varied widely. A few respondents singled out individual parole officers who they regarded as sympathetic and helpful to their progress.

The respondents feared more prison time if they violated their parole. JO, who was required to enter drug treatment while on parole although he had been in multiple treatment programs put it this way: "*If I look at someone wrong I can get picked up.*" A 38-year-old man, RL, who had already been incarcerated on four separate drug-related offenses, said he would rather serve his full sentence in prison rather than on parole, *"because being on parole is too hard, you know? They come to my mom's house at five in the morning. They say I can't have my dog. They said the knife on my mom's kitchen counter is too long."* Likewise, FZ, a 41-year-old homeless man who served four sentences for drug sales and possession charges, was living with his girlfriend's friend in public housing, *"The girl I'm staying with gets high on cocaine and heroin. A friend of mine says I gotta get out of there because everyone knows she uses."*

A few respondents described being torn between family and parole obligations. One man said that he stayed away from his ex-wife and their two sons because the boys were smoking marijuana. During the discussion with PHR/Fortune interviewers, it became clear that he was less afraid of using the drug himself (he had been addicted to cocaine and alcohol) than of disobeying parole: *"If I didn't have this predicate bid, I wouldn't think twice about seeing my kids. My parole officer told me 'You can't let nothing jeopardize your freedom. It took me three weeks to tell my wife why I can't go by – because of my sons' marijuana. She blew up.... As much as I love my wife and sons I can't take that risk.... If I go to prison I would die."*

Some respondents voiced frustration that parole was not more helpful to them in finding work as ex-prisoners. For example, RH, a 43-year-old man who was charged with parole violations four times following his release from a drug sale prison sentence, said that he had hoped that his parole officer would help him find employment but was disappointed: *"They really don't try to do anything else [other than supervision] for you. They don't try to help you with employment like they are supposed to."* This negative view of parole spirals into blanket condemnation: *"I always thought parole was there to help you, but it's a business... they're just there to keep you coming back. They have all sorts of resources and things for ex-offenders that they don't give you."*

* * * * *

One could argue that the people interviewed for this study had little reason to maintain the optimism that they expressed. Most had experienced the difficulties of negotiating relationships with disappointed parents, siblings, partners and children in the past, as well as learned the value of the support gained from these same people. Most had struggled to find stable housing and many continued that struggle. Most had applied for jobs and been refused because of lack of practical or social skills or because of the stigma of a criminal record. Many struggled to understand how to make the most of lives they felt ashamed of knowing that their health was not good and aware that they might die relatively young. And yet respondents overwhelmingly were optimistic, offering an indication of the resolve and potential that they offer if they do what so many said they wanted to do: stay out of trouble.

VII. EXISTING ALTERNATIVES

Types of Drug Treatment

Drug treatment can roughly be divided into (private) fee-based programs and publicly-funded programs, which offer roughly the same range of treatment interventions. Drug treatment for people in the criminal justice system parallels publicly-funded treatment for the general population.

In general, both privately and publicly funded treatment range from short-term interventions involving no more than detoxification over a period of two days to long-term interventions of up to two years. Detoxification programs are generally designed as triage or preliminary care and are not expected to stop drug abuse on their own. Some treatment programs are outpatient, with length and amount of programming varying from a few hours each week to the equivalent of a full-time job. The programs that are generally considered the most effective involve residential treatment, typically lasting at least nine months.[75] However, it is important to note that few studies have compared treatment designs such as outpatient and residential formats, and some researchers and advocates have suggested that the flexibility of outpatient treatment is more effective for some. Likewise, while public and private treatment options share many goals, there are few studies comparing them structurally, in content or in outcome. It is clear, however, that private treatment facilities are generally more accommodating to participants than those public options serving indigent participants.[76] This is an important issue when considering how to achieve successful treatment outcomes given the high rate of treatment dropout and the importance of early retention in treatment for maintaining sobriety.

---

[75] Lawrence Sherman, Denise Gottfredson, Doris MacKenzie, John Eck, Peter Reuter & Shawn Bushway. *Preventing Crime: What Works, What Doesn't and What's Promising.* Washington, D.C.: National Institute of Justice. 1998. Gerald Gaes, Timothy Flanagan, Lawrence Motiuk & Lynn Stewart. "Adult Correctional Treatment" in, Michael Tonry & Joan Petersilia, ed.'s. *Crime and Justice.* Vol. 26. Chicago: University of Chicago. 1999. Douglas Lipton. *The Effectiveness of Treatment for Drug Abusers Under Criminal Justice Supervision.* Washington, D.C.: National Institute of Justice. 1995. These results may reflect that research for residential drug treatment has been funded at higher levels and is generally easier to complete because of data availability than is research on outpatient programs.

[76] For example see Hazelden's website which points out to prospective clients that their "accommodations, meals and recreational facilities rate among the finest resorts." http://hazelden.com

Generally, drug treatment programs involve a combination of peer-support and reaction, counseling, cognitive skill development and 12-step (based on Alcoholics Anonymous) philosophy. While research indicates that some of these elements are linked with positive results, much remains unknown about the relationship of these elements- individually and in combination to successful drug use cessation. The treatment programs that exist were designed largely in response to the heroin epidemic of the 1970s and the crack epidemic of the 1980s. As drug use patterns change, it is unclear whether the content and structure of treatment should change as well. In New York, increasing numbers of people entering the criminal justice system report that marijuana is their primary drug.[77] The combination of marijuana, cocaine and heroin users in a single treatment program may complicate treatment delivery for programs because of different patterns of use and addiction associated with each drug.

The Cycle of Addiction, Recidivism and the Criminal Justice System

Judges, defense attorneys, advocates and even prosecutors acknowledge that many of those who fill the New York courts have been there before and will return, because they continue to use the drugs that make legal employment and a stable lifestyle difficult to establish and maintain.

For example, a report by an independent commission created by Chief Judge of the State of New York Judith S. Kaye addressed the problem of nonviolent drug addicts whose drug and drug-related crimes are motivated by addiction. The report noted that recidivism rates are high for people convicted of drug felony offenses. Of those released from state prison in 1996, 56 percent were rearrested within three years and over two-thirds were rearrested for new drug crimes.[78] The commission estimated that in 1999, as many as 10,000 nonviolent addicted criminal defendants who could have been eligible for treatment alternatives to incarceration were instead sentenced to jail or state prison.[79]

In general, the majority of inmates have had poor access to healthcare prior to incarceration.[80] As such, many have not been in drug treatment before and therefore first enter drug treatment through the doorway of

---

[77] Rachel Porter, Mary Ludz & Sophia Lee. *Balancing Punishment and Treatment: Alternatives to Incarceration in New York*. New York: Vera Institute of Justice. 2002.

[78] New York State Commission on Drugs and the Courts. *Confronting the Cycle of Addiction and Recidivism: A Report to Chief Judge Judith S. Kaye*. June 2000. Accessed on March 2, 2004 at www.nycourts.gov/reports/addictionrecidivism.shtml

[79] *Confronting the Cycle of Addiction and Recidivism: A Report to Chief Judge Judith S. Kaye.*

[80] National Commission on Correctional Health Care. *The Health Status of Soon-to-be-Released Inmates: A Report to Congress*. March 2002, vol. 1, p. 4.

the criminal justice system as a consequence of arrest and referral through the courts.

Mandated drug treatment may take the place of incarceration and is monitored by court or court-specified authorities. Some of these alternatives are described in more detail further in this section (see below). Mandated drug treatment may take one of several forms (i.e. modalities) including residential drug treatment or outpatient drug treatment. Different modalities of drug treatment may also be available to some inmates within a prison or local jail, however such treatment is voluntary (although arguably participation is based on coercion). The intensity and quality of drug treatment varies across treatment modality for both in-prison and out of prison programs.

Debates about the utility of coerced treatment have generally concluded that it does not result in worse treatment outcomes and may, in fact, result in better outcomes than voluntary treatment.[81] A defendant or inmate may be more likely to enter drug treatment because of the crisis of being arrested and may be more likely to stay in treatment given the negative consequence of imprisonment. It is important to note that some advocates oppose coerced treatment under the principle that people should not be forced into drug treatment. They note that failure rates may be exacerbated if participants are suspicious of treatment providers linked to the corrections system and these treatment providers may lose all but the least severe addicts to flight or incarceration. But, beyond this debate, there is a dearth of available drug abuse treatment slots in New York where national estimates of the number of people in need of treatment are estimated at some 3 percent of the state's population.[82]

A frequently made assumption in drug treatment is that "relapse is part of recovery" – i.e. that most people trying to overcome addiction will use drugs at some point in their effort to remain abstinent.[83] This knowledge is commonplace in other public health efforts, for example an overweight person on a calorie restricted diet who sneaks a forbidden candy bar, or a person who requires several attempts before successfully quitting

---

[81] David Farabee, Michael Pendergast & Douglas Anglin. "The Effectiveness of Coerced Treatment for Drug Abusing Offenders." *Federal Probation*. Vol. 62, no. 1. 1998. pp. 3-10. Matthew Hiller, Kevin Knight, Kirn Broome & Dwayne Simpson. "Legal Pressure and Treatment Retention in a National Sample of Long-Term Residential Programs." *Criminal Justice and Behavior*. Vol. 25, no.4. 1998. p. 463-481

[82] Douglas Wright. *State Estimates of Substance Abuse from the 2001 National Household Survey on Drug Abuse*. Washington, D.C.: Department of Health and Human Services. 2003. http://www.samhsa.gov/centers/clearinghouse/clearinghouses.html

[83] Douglas Anglin & Yih-Ing Hser. *Criminal Justice and the Drug-Abusing Offender: Policy Issues of Coerced Treatment*. Drug Abuse Research Group. University of California, Los Angeles. 1990. Robert MacCoun and Peter Reuter. *Drug War Heresies: Learning from Other Vices, Times, & Places*. Cambridge University Press. New York. 2001.

cigarettes. The consequences of relapse for a drug user, however, are more significant. A person who is trying to stop using drugs commits a crime at each relapse. If that person is on parole supervision, he or she can be returned to prison for months or years for such a parole violation.

Alternatives to Incarceration

Some people convicted of drug offenses in New York avoid prison sentences through alternative to incarceration programs (ATIs) available in several counties in New York. ATI programs combine the coercive power of the court with the therapeutic intervention of a direct service program. A defendant agrees to plead guilty to a crime, enter a treatment program (usually residential), agree to an alternative sentence for failure to engage in the treatment, and, in exchange, the prosecutor and the court agree to waive a jail or prison sentence if the defendant successfully completes treatment. Usually ATI programs are offered to defendants charged with drug crimes who are in need of drug treatment and who are not accused of violent offenses. Some ATIs are available for people who do not need drug treatment and others are also open to people accused of violent crimes. Because the prosecutor agrees to an ATI, the sentence may be used instead of the mandatory incarceration stipulated by the Rockefeller drug laws.

Alternatives to incarceration are provided through drug courts, direct service providers and prosecution-based programs. These alternatives aim to increase individual responsibility and the humanity of the penal system while decreasing reoffending and reducing the costs associated with incarceration. Many of the ATIs tailor their services to the individual needs of their clients, and therefore address a range of social needs beyond rehabilitation including education, healthcare, parenting and job development. Policy makers, treatment providers and criminal justice experts have lauded several of the ATIs described in this report, yet all are underutilized because of funding limitations and structural impediments established by mandatory sentencing laws.

New York City has an extensive network of ATIs relative to the rest of the state
and in comparison with other states. There are several kinds of ATIs operating in the city: drug courts, independent, direct service provider-run ATIs, and Drug Treatment Alternatives to Prison (DTAP). There are also "boot camp"-style programs that incorporate residence in a quasi-military style boot camp along with extended supervision upon completion of the boot camp session. These options are listed, below, in ascending order of the general severity of the criminal conviction of their client population.

Drug Courts

The first drug court opened in Miami in 1989. Drug courts began to operate in New York in 1995 in Brooklyn. Currently there are six drug courts in the five boroughs of New York City and throughout the rest of the state. Most drug courts are for first-time felony offenders only, but some serve misdemeanor offenders and second-time felony offenders as well. Federal funding requirements prohibit drug courts from serving violent offenders. The structure of these courts is to perform a clinical evaluation of an offender and determine if drug abuse or addiction was the precipitator of the crime that is before the court. If it is determined so, the offender is given the opportunity to enter treatment rather than incarceration.

A drug court is an alternate court partly devoted to taking pleas to predetermined drug offenses and levels (for example, possession with intent to sell in the third degree). Unlike traditional courtrooms, the drug court is designed to maximize interaction between the defendant and the judge. The defendant agrees to enter treatment and return to court every two weeks for supervision by the judge. In exchange, the charge against the defendant is dropped or reduced upon successful completion of treatment. The prosecutor and defense agree to the terms of the drug court during the planning of the hearing, and are present while court is in session. Unlike a traditional criminal court, however, the judge speaks directly to the defendant and it is that contact that is considered a critical element of the court's engagement with the person charged with a drug crime. Drug courts are constructed as teams made up of all court parties including the defendant who, it is postulated, must be motivated to stop drug use in order to also stop drug-related offending. Once the defendant agrees to the drug court plea, she or he enters one of the drug treatment programs with which the court works. Some drug courts have connections to dozens of such treatment programs, others work with only one or two. While residential drug treatment may be available for drug court participants, the courts in New York rely on outpatient treatment that ranges from nonintensive to full-time (35 hours/week).

One public defender in the Bronx, however, has voiced concerns about drug courts providing real alternatives to incarceration. In the case of the Bronx drug court, first time felony drug offenders over the age of 19 are eligible. But those who enter the drug court, at least in the Bronx, would not always have received a sentence of incarceration prior to the inception of the drug court:

> *... at least one attorney has told me that nearly every person charged with first-time felony drug crimes was offered probation prior to the inception of the drug treatment court in the Bronx. In my experience,*

however, those clients who decline drug treatment court as an option are not always offered probation. Thus, to call the Bronx Treatment Court an alternative to incarceration for first-time felony drug offenders may be somewhat off the mark.[84]

The public defender also stated that to participate in drug treatment court, most defendants must agree to a promised sentence of two to six years of incarceration even though the statutory minimum for the charge to which they are pleading is a term of one to three years.[85]

Direct Service Provider Alternative to Incarceration Programs

New York City has dozens of non-profit and for-profit social service agencies which specifically target or are willing to work with people convicted of drug crimes and ex-prisoners. A number of these programs operate specifically as alternatives to incarceration (ATIs), working independently in the criminal and supreme courts to convince defendants, attorneys and judges that a defendant and the public would be better served through the ATI than through incarceration.

These programs have their own eligibility criteria and their own programming which is typically a combination of counseling, skill development and social services that is specified according to individual need. The programs are almost always full-time outpatient. As with DTAP and with drug courts, the sentencing judge monitors defendants who enter ATIs on a regular basis, typically once a month. However ATIs, rather than the defendant, present reports to the judge and there is very limited or no interaction between the judge and the defendant. Generally a defendant agrees to a plea but sentencing is delayed until after completion of the ATI at which point a non incarcerative sentence is imposed. In cases in which a mandatory sentence is required by law, the defendant is allowed to withdraw his guilty plea to a felony and enter a plea to a misdemeanor so that a non-custodial sentence can be imposed.

New York City has a unique community of dedicated, non-profit ATI providers who have helped to foster an atmosphere of productive debate about alternatives to traditional criminal justice policies. In order to displace incarceration, the programs typically target serious felony offenders whose crimes in many instances are covered by mandatory sentences, i.e. who would otherwise be sentenced to prison or jail. The programs, in such cases, must rely on prosecutors to accept the ATI sentence. Partly because

---

[84] Mae C. Quinn, "Whose Team Am I on Anyway? Musings of a Public Defender about Drug Treatment Court Practice," *New York University School of Law Review of Law and Social Change*, v. 26 (2000/2001), p. 61, n. 140.

[85] Quinn, p. 62. See also Rachel Porter. *Treatment Alternatives in the Criminal Court: A Process Evaluation of the Bronx County Drug Court. Report to the Criminal Court of the City of New York.* New York: Vera Institute of Justice. 2001.

of prosecutorial reluctance to use the ATIs for serious offenders and because of program capacity due to budgets, the programs are underused.

"Boot Camp" Alternatives:

There are "boot camp" alternatives to prison that combine a period of incarceration in a military-style camp facility rather than a traditional prison, with subsequent parole supervision. For example, New York's Department of Correctional Services operates a six-month "Shock Incarceration" program, designed for people convicted of a felony who may have a prior felony conviction, but are serving their first prison sentence. It combines academic instruction, substance abuse education, and group and individual counseling. This intensive program is then followed by six months of intensive parole supervision. Although Shock is not strictly a drug treatment program, it does permit some offenders sentenced to mandatory time for drug offenses to leave prison early.[86]

New York also offers the Willard Drug Treatment Program designed for low-level second-felony drug offenders who have no violent or "serious" (class A or B felony) prior convictions. Participants are sent into a secure, 90-day, treatment phase with a quasi-military boot camp component and then go into at least six months of community-based treatment. In addition, there is an Extended Willard program, which New York State hoped would make the program more attractive to prosecutors by extending the period of supervision that participants must undergo. The extended version includes an additional six months in community-based residential treatment between the boot camp and outpatient phases of the original Willard design. The Vera Institute for Justice conducted a study that showed that New York was "filling less than half of the treatment capacity provided by the state, continuing to send most offenders with Willard-eligible criminal records to prison, despite the available alternative."[87]

Concern has been raised about the effectiveness of boot camp alternatives. One multi-state study showed that in three states – Illinois, Louisiana, and New York – boot camp graduates may have had lower recidivism rates on particular recidivism measures, but this was because these states included an intensive post-boot camp supervision phase for graduates. The authors concluded that "results clearly show that the core elements of boot

---

[86] James Wilson, Steven Wood, Robert Hope, Kajal Gehi. *The Challenges of Replacing Prison with Drug Treatment*. Vera Institute for Justice. September 2003.

[87] Wilson, et al. *The Challenges of Replacing Prison with Drug Treatment*.

[88] Doris Layton MacKenzie and Claire Souryal, "Multisite Study of Correctional Boot Camps." In *Correctional Boot Camps: A Tough Intermediate Sanction*. Doris Layton MacKenzie and Eugene E. Hebert, eds. National Institute of Justice Report, February 1996. See also Dale Parent "Correctional Boot Camps: Lessons from a Decade of Research" 2003. NIJ. http://www.ojp.usdoj.gov/nij/pubs-sum/197018.htm

camp programs – military-style discipline, hard labor, and physical training – by themselves did not reduce offender recidivism."[88]

Drug Treatment Alternatives to Prison (DTAP)

The DTAP program was started by the Kings County (Brooklyn) District Attorney's (DA) (prosecutor) office in 1990 in order to divert second-time felony drug offenders from the mandatory prison sentences specified under the Rockefeller statute.[89] The DA works with New York State residential drug treatment programs called "therapeutic communities" to combine long-term residential drug treatment with court-based supervision. Therapeutic communities generally follow a three-phase model. Each phase lasts approximately six months and gradually moves the participant from a highly structured and supervised lifestyle to greater autonomy and personal responsibility. In the first phase, the participant lives in a group residence frequently located outside of the city and is prohibited from leaving the facility or from receiving telephone calls or visits during the initial weeks of treatment. Treatment in this phase consists of group and individual discussion, confrontation and counseling. Participants have chores, and required, scheduled meals, activities and therapy sessions.

As a participant progresses he or she moves to phase two and another residential facility closer to home. Treatment in this phase generally involves educational and vocational development as well as continued drug abuse counseling, increased contact with family members, and development as a peer mentor for newer participants. In phase three the participant generally lives at home, attends an outpatient drug treatment therapy group, receives individual counseling, and is monitored for drug use, class attendance and other indicators of developed responsibility.

Throughout the period that a DTAP participant is required to attend treatment, the treatment provider or an intermediary organization provides monthly reports to the sentencing judge about the person's progress in treatment. The participant is generally present in court for each report. The theory behind these reports is two-fold. In terms of the therapeutic value of court reporting, the regular appearance before the judge in the courtroom is thought to remind the participant that treatment is required and that leaving treatment would result in incarceration – essentially coercing the participant to remain in treatment regardless of how little innate desire he or she has to stop using drugs for good. In terms of criminal justice process, the regular court reports are considered a means of demonstrating concern for the public safety by regularly monitoring the conduct of those convicted of drug crimes who are not incarcerated.

---

[89] DTAP programs are run by local prosecutors. For information on the Brooklyn DTAP program, see Charles Hynes, Anne Swern and David Heslin, *Drug Treatment Alternatives to Prison: 10th Annual Report.* NY: District Attorney's Office of King's County. 2000.

Started by a prosecutor and now operated by prosecutors in each of New York City's five jurisdictions, DTAP is regarded as the most acceptable treatment-based sentence by prosecutors[90] for two reasons. First, DTAP requires that participants agree to lengthened incarceration periods should they fail in DTAP. This means that a defendant agreeing to enter DTAP also agrees to a 2-4-year prison term without any further sentence reduction through plea-bargaining if he or she fails to complete DTAP. Second, residential and long-term drug treatment is seen as appropriately restrictive to use as a sentence for a crime, a proportionality which many prosecutors find lacking in outpatient and short-term treatment.

Important Caveats to Alternatives to Incarceration

There are some serious concerns with court-mandated alternative sentences. Sometimes a "widening of the net" of criminal justice supervision may occur, which means that the court may impose treatment mandates upon low-level drug offenders that are longer than the penalties they would face absent such programs, for example probation with no incarceration or a short period of jail time. In addition, since there is a very high failure rate in drug treatment, a mandate to complete treatment, with a threat of incarceration upon failure to do so, poses the risk that incarceration will be imposed on individuals who would not have been incarcerated but for the existence of the alternative. Following that, there is the risk that the drug court or other intervention may impose harsher penalties upon those who fail treatment than upon those who simply take the originally offered prison sentence. Finally, it is also important to note that alternative sentences typically do involve waiving the right to trial and accepting a guilty plea, which would put defendants in the position of being vulnerable to more severe sentences should they be charged again in the future.

In considering these alternative sentences, it is important to note that they currently account for only a fraction of felony sentences in the state, that the state's current ATI capacity is far below the possible number of cases for which they could be used, and that ATI options and opportunities vary widely depending on the county.[91] While research about these

---

[90] See Young *et al*, 1998.

[91] There is no reliable source of information for the total number of ATIs used in lieu of a sentence in the state as a whole. The New York City Criminal Justice Agency reported that 1,014 entered the seven primary ATI programs funded by the New York City Criminal Justice Coordinator during a 15 month period from the March 1998 through mid-2000. See, Mary Phillips, Aida Tejaratchi, Wayne Nehwaowich, Raymond Caligiure, Taehyon Kim, Elizabeth Walton & Bernice Linen-Reed. *Estimating Jail Displacement for Alternative-To-Incarceration Programs in New York City.* New York: New York City Criminal Justice Agency. 2002

programs is ongoing and measures of success vary, researchers are generally optimistic about the ability of alternative programs to reduce reoffending at a lower cost than incarceration.

VIII. THE WAR ON DRUGS IN THE UNITED STATES

Out of concern that drug abuse in America was spiraling out of control, there were a number of responses at the national and state levels in the early 1970s, with New York's Rockefeller drug laws among the more draconian measures.

At the national level, the Nixon Administration initiated the first "war on drugs," when, in 1971, Nixon set up the Special Action Office for Drug Abuse Prevention to coordinate national drug policy and prevent the importation of illegal substances. Additional measures included the 1970 Comprehensive Drug Abuse Prevention and Control Act, which consolidated prior anti-drug legislation and made legal distinctions among banned drugs based on their perceived harmfulness. The Act also provided federal support for programs aimed at preventing and treating drug abuse; indeed, the Nixon Administration placed more emphasis on "demand reduction," or prevention and treatment, than later administrations. Nixon also created the Drug Enforcement Administration (DEA) in place of several anti-drug agencies in 1973.[92]

The Reagan Administration transformed the war on drugs into one focusing more on law enforcement than drug abuse prevention and treatment. This effort was initiated by key administration officials such as FBI Director William Webster, Attorney General William Smith and Secretary of Education and later "Drug Czar" William Bennett, who believed that drugs were a national security threat and should be prioritized as such by law enforcement.[93]

The Reagan Administration's war on drugs oversaw the launch of a combined strategy of budgetary allocation and new laws. Unfortunately "the war" never prioritized mobilizing doctors and public health workers to reduce demand for illegal drugs. The government cut funding for public agencies targeting drug abuse through treatment options, such as the National Institute on Drug Abuse (launched by the Nixon Administration) and other programs aimed at reducing poverty and degradation, such as child nutrition programs.[94] Meanwhile, fiscal allocation to law enforce-

---

[92] For more on the early history of drug and alcohol policy in America, see David Musto, ed. *Drugs in America: A Documentary History*. New York: NYU Press. 2002.

[93] Michael Massing. *The Fix*. New York: Simon and Schuster. 1998.

[94] Katherine Beckett and Theodore Sasson. *The Politics of Injustice: Crime and Punishment on America* Thousand Oaks, Ca.: Sage Publications. 2000.

ment agencies including the Federal Bureau of Investigation, the Drug Enforcement Agency and the Defense Department were increased substantially and described as necessary in order to address the supply side of the drug market.[95]

These new fiscal priorities were joined by legislative actions that increased the severity of punishment for drug related crimes, most evident by three new laws. First, in 1986, President Reagan signed the Anti-Drug Abuse Act[96] into law, mandating minimum sentences for some drug offenses, permitting capital punishment for some drug offenses, weakening regulations about admissible evidence and, perhaps most critically, establishing a sentence differential of 100 times greater severity of punishment for cocaine in its cheap and potent rock form – crack – than in its more expensive powder form. Second, in 1988, this act was expanded to include more mandatory minimum sentences at the federal level. Then, in 1994, President Clinton signed the Violent Crime Control and Law Enforcement Act[97] into law, increasing funds allocated to law enforcement and prison construction, increasing many mandatory and permissible sentences and further limiting inmates' rights.

Together these efforts defined drug use and abuse as a critical threat to public safety. Stories of crack-addicted psychopaths permeated public consciousness through both political rhetoric and media outlets.[98] The result was a national demonization of drug use, which steered the war on drugs towards a focus on poor, disenfranchised and minority drug users, who were unlikely to have political or media influence.

Nationally, the numbers of white drug users exceeds that of African-American users, and drug use among whites has remained relatively stable as it has among African-Americans.[99] The war on drugs, however, has led to a rate of arrest of African-American users nearly eight times that of arrest of white users.[100] While national data from the early 1990s demonstrated that whites make up 76 percent of illicit drug users, African-Americans, 14 percent and Latinos 8 percent, African-Americans account for

---

[95]See for example, Marc Mauer. *Race to Incarcerate*. The New Press. 1999.

[96] Public Law 99-570.

[97] Public Law 103-322.

[98] Craig Reinarman & Harry Levine. "Crack in Context" in Craig Reinarman & Harry Levine, ed.s *Crack in America* Berkeley: University of California Press. 1997.

[99] Substance Abuse and Mental Health Services Administration (SAMHSA). *Summary of Findings from the 2000 National Household Survey on Drug Abuse*. Washington, DC: Department of Health and Human Services, 2000 and SAMHSA, 1998 National Household Survey on Drug Abuse.

[100] Bruce Western, Becky Pettit & Josh Guetzkow. "Black Economic Progress in the Era of Mass Imprisonment" in Marc Mauer & Meda Chesney-Lind, ed.s *Invisible Punishment*. New York: The New Press. 2002. See also, Paige Harrison & Aleenen Beck. *Prisoners in 2002*. Bureau of Justice Statistics, U.S. Department of Justice. Washington D.C. 2003.

35 percent of drug arrests in that period, 55 percent of all convictions and 74 percent of all sentences for drug offenses.[101] According to the noted criminologist Norval Morris: "The whole law and order movement that we have heard so much about is, in operation though not in intent, anti-black and anti-underclass."[102]

This pattern of selective enforcement has continued as has research on the prevalence of drug use, which demonstrates that minority communities are disproportionately targeted by these laws.[103] According to one analysis: "The contrast between the ethnic distribution of drug users in the community and in drug treatment, medical or other institutional samples illustrates clearly that the treated and clinical population do not constitute a representative sample of users and abusers in the community."[104] By targeting street-level drug sales, the war on drugs is also a war on the communities where drugs are sold on the street as opposed to in homes, clubs, and other private locations to which the police would have a harder time gaining entry and which are largely the domain of the more affluent.

Today the Office of National Drug Control Policy continues to prioritize law enforcement over targeted prevention and education, spending more than half of its projected budget of 11.7 million dollars for fiscal year 2004 on enforcement in Defense, Homeland Security, Justice, State Department activities and other government agencies. The budgetary explanation does not include reference to poverty reduction or other infrastructure needs that characterize drug users involved in the criminal justice system.[105]

As a result of this law enforcement approach to drug addiction, the number of people incarcerated in the nation's jails and prisons has grown from approximately 500,000 people in 1980 to over 2 million in 2002,[106] and the number of people under community supervision – either parole or probation – has jumped to over 4 million.[107] The United States incarcerates more of its citizens than any other country.[108]

---

[101] David Cole. *No Equal Justice: Race and Class in the American Criminal Justice System.* New York: The New Press. 1999.

[102] Norval Morris. "Race and Crime: What Evidence is there that Race Influences Results in the Criminal Justice System? *Judicature.* Vol. 72, no. 2. 1988.

[103] Michael Tonry. *Malign Neglect.* New York: Oxford University Press. 1995.

[104] Denise Kandel. "Social Demography of Drug Use" in Ronald Bayer and Gerald Oppenheimer, eds. *Confronting Drug Policy: Illicit Drugs in a Free Society.* Cambridge University Press: New York. 1993. p. 69. See also, the National Household Survey on Drug Abuse: http://www.samhsa.gov/oas/nhsda.htm#NHSDAinfo.

[105] Office of National Drug Control Policy. Projected Budget 2004. http://whitehousedrugpolicy.gov/

[106] See Bureau of Justice Statistics. "Key Facts at a Glance: Correctional Populations." Accessible at: http://www.ojp.usdoj.gov/bjs/glance/tables/corr2tab.htm

[107] At the end of 2002, over 4.7 million adult men and women were under Federal, State, or local probation or parole jurisdiction, see Lauren E. Glaze. *Probation and Parole in the United States, 2002.* Bureau of Justice Statistics. August 2003.

[108] "A Nation Behind Bars." (Editorial). *The Washington Post.* April 13, 2003, B6.

IX. APPLICATION OF RELEVANT INTERNATIONAL AND DOMESTIC LAWS

United States Law

United States Constitutional Law: The Eighth Amendment

The US Constitution's Eighth Amendment states that, "Excessive bail shall not be required, nor excessive fines imposed, nor cruel and unusual punishments inflicted."[109] This section describes the challenges faced by people convicted of drug crimes in appealing the length of sentences and poor treatment in prison under the Eighth Amendment.

For the problem of lengthy sentences for offenses (such as the Rockefeller drug laws' mandatory minimum sentences), legal scholars often focus on interpreting the Eighth Amendment through the lens of proportionality[110]: whether the punishment fits the crime and whether lengthy sentences for nonviolent drug offenses might be considered "cruel and unusual."

The US Supreme Court has gone back and forth on whether to support a proportionality review on sentences in non-capital cases as shown in two conflicting high court cases. In *Solem v. Helm*[111] in 1983, the Court held that there was a proportionality guarantee between a crime and its punishment implicit in the Eighth Amendment. However, in *Harmelin v. Michigan*[112] in 1991, the Court held that the Eighth Amendment does not guarantee proportionality.[113] Further, the Court in *Harmelin* held that courts should grant substantial deference to state legislatures in punishing their offenders and writing sentencing statutes.

---

[109] See the Law Library of Congress's online resources on the Constitution, available at http://www.loc.gov/law/guide/usconst.html.

[110] See for example William H. Mulligan, "Cruel and Unusual Punishments: The Proportionality Rule," 47 *Fordham L. Rev.* 639, 642 (1979), Paula C. Johnson, "At the Intersection of Injustice: Experiences of African American Women in Crime and Sentencing" 4 Am. U. J. *Gender & Law* 1 (1995), and Martin A. Greer, "Human Rights and Wrongs in Our Own Backyard: Incorporating International Human Rights Protections Under Domestic Civil Rights Law" 13 *Harv. Hum. Rts. J.* 71 (2000).

[111] *Solem v. Helm*, 463 U.S. 277 (1983).

[112] *Harmelin v. Michigan*, 501 U.S. 957 (1991).

[113] Two Justices found *Helm* wrong and that no proportionality guarantee exists; three concurred but found it existed only if the sentence was first found to be "grossly disproportionate"; and four dissented, indicating their belief that there was a proportionality guarantee in all cases: *Harmelin v. Michigan*, 501 U.S. 957 (1991).

Again deferring to state legislatures, in 2003 the Supreme Court rejected two Eighth Amendment challenges to "cruel and unusual" sentences. In *Ewing v. California*[114] and *Andrade v. Lockyer*,[115] the high court rejected challenges to the application of California's harsh "Three Strikes and You're Out" law to recidivist defendants found guilty of nonviolent, relatively minor offenses and given lengthy prison sentences.[116]

Civil Rights of Institutionalized Persons Act and the Prisoner Litigation Reform Act

Once incarcerated, prisoners face new obstacles should they wish to challenge poor conditions or abusive treatment in prison. Prisoners' constitutional rights may be enforced by the Department of Justice (DOJ) via civil suits under the Civil Rights of Institutionalized Persons Act[117]or criminal enforcement under the US Code.[118] But, as Human Rights Watch stated in its 2001 report on male rape in US prisons, "All of these statutes are... subject to prosecutorial discretion. The DOJ has no affirmative obligation to enforce them in every instance, nor, it should be emphasized, does it have the resources to do so."[119] In addition, there is also the burden of intent; not only must prosecutors prove that a prisoner's constitutional rights have been violated, but that there was "specific intent" to violate them.[120]

Thus the most common way to challenge poor conditions and abusive treatment is for prisoners to file civil litigation to claim that state officials deprived them of their constitutional rights.[121] In 1996, however, in a move designed to limit so-called frivolous lawsuits by the incarcerated, Congress restricted the ability of prisoners to sue for constitutional rights violations through the Prisoner Litigation Reform Act (PLRA).[122]

---

[114] *Ewing v. California*, 123 S. Ct. 1179 (2003).

[115] Andrade v. Lockyer, 123 S. Ct. 1166 (2003).

[116] In *Ewing*, the defendant received a 25-years-to-life term for shoplifting golf clubs; in *Andrade*, the defendant received a 50-years-to-life sentence for the theft of videotapes. See Laurie L. Levenson, "Picking up the Slack," *National Law Journal*, vol. 25, no. 48, August 18, 2003, 33.

[117] Civil Rights of Institutionalized Persons Act, Public Law 96-247, 42 U.S.C. 1997.

[118] Sections 241 and 242 of Title 18 of the U.S. Code. Section 241 prohibits conspiracies to deprive any person of civil rights secured by the Constitution or U.S. law. Section 242 prohibits those acting under color of law from depriving persons of civil rights secured by the Constitution or U.S. law. See Marshall Miller, "Police Brutality," 17 *Yale L. & Pol'y Rev.*, 153 (1998).

[119] See Human Rights Watch, *No Escape: Male Rape in U.S. Prisons* (New York: HRW, April 2001), http://www.hrw.org/reports/2001/prison/report.html.

[120] Miller, 153.

[121] Under Section 1983 of Title 42 of the U.S. Code.

[122] Prison Litigation Reform Act of 1995, Public Law No. 104-134, 110 Stat. 1321-66 (1996).

For example, the PLRA bars litigation for mental or emotional injury to prisoners in the absence of physical injury.[123] The statute also requires indigent prisoners, unlike any other indigent federal court civil litigants, to pay the entire court filing fee even though prisoners are among the most impoverished categories of people in the United States.[124] In addition, the PLRA requires that in order for prisoners to challenge living conditions in prison they must first exhaust the institution's administrative remedies. As noted by the director of the Prisoners' Rights Project of the New York Legal Aid Society, "applied to the mostly uneducated, unsophisticated, and legally uncounseled population of the prisons, the requirement invites technical mistakes resulting in inadvertent non-compliance with the exhaustion requirement."[125] The PLRA has, therefore, levied what may be viewed as steep barriers to prisoners seeking protection of their constitutional rights.

International Human Rights Law

The Rockefeller drug laws appear to be contrary to standards set forth in international instruments, including ones that have been ratified by the United States.

These sentences violate international standards as set forth in the Universal Declaration of Human Rights[126] and in international treaties such as the International Covenant on Civil and Political Rights (ICCPR)[127] and the Convention Against Torture and Other Cruel, Inhuman, or Degrading Treatment or Punishment (CAT).[128] The ICCPR and the CAT, both ratified by the United States[129], maintain the right of all individuals, including those convicted of a crime, to be free of cruel, inhuman and degrading treatment or punishment, without derogation.[130] While fundamental rights

---

[123] For an overview of the PLRA, see John Boston, "The Prison Litigation Reform Act: The New Face of Court Stripping" 67 *Brooklyn L. Rev.* (Winter 2001), 429. For the section prohibiting suits for mental or emotional injury without physical injury, see 42 U.S.C. § 1997e(e).

[124] Boston, 429.

[125] Boston, 429.

[126] Universal Declaration of Human Rights, G.A. res. 217A (III), U.N. Doc A/810 at 71 (1948).

[127] International Covenant on Civil and Political Rights, United Nations G.A. Res. 2200a (XXI), UN GAOR, 21st Sess., Supp. no 16., UN Doc A/6316 (1967), entry into force March 23, 1976.

[128] Convention against Torture and Other Cruel, Inhuman or Degrading Treatment or Punishment, G.A. res. 39/46, [annex, 39 U.N. GAOR Supp. (No. 51) at 197, U.N. Doc. A/39/51 (1984)], entry into force June 26, 1987.

[129] The United States ratified the ICCPR in 1992 and the CAT in 1994.

[130] ICCPR (Article 7) and CAT (Article16).

such as freedom of speech and freedom of mobility may be restricted in prison, prisoners are under state protection during incarceration, and the state must ensure that they are not harassed through humiliating or intimidating behavior or images, or placed at increased risk of rape and other abuses.[131]

In addition to the provisions in international treaties, prison standards were discussed in detail by the United Nations' Standard Minimum Rules for the Treatment of Prisoners (adopted in 1957), which describe the minimum prison conditions which are accepted as suitable by the United Nations. It is notable that these rules emphasize that the ultimate purpose of incarceration is rehabilitation and reintegration into society. Thus, for example, "From the beginning of a prisoner's sentence, consideration shall be given to future release, and the prisoner needs to be assisted in maintaining social relations outside the institution."[132] In addition, the furtherance of rehabilitation and reintegration must happen in tandem with medical care and treatment.[133] International legal norms, therefore, appear to emphasize rehabilitation and reintegration into society much more so than does U.S. domestic law.[134]

International human rights law, however, is rarely used in the US legal system. In order to be justiciable in US courts, provisions of such treaties must be passed as domestic US law. In addition, the US frequently makes use of reservations/declarations in order to exempt it from international enforcement mechanisms and other provisions it finds objectionable.[135] For example, the US has ratified the ICCPR, but made it clear through its reservations to the ICCPR that it considers itself exempt from the treaty's enforcement methods among other specific ICCPR provisions.[136] The US ratified the Convention Against Torture, but has only implemented it to a limited extent. Indeed, "The limiting provisions that the US attached to its

---

[131] See Amnesty International, "Violations in Prisons and Jails: Needless Brutality," in *RIGHTS FOR ALL* (1998), available at http://www.rightsforall-usa.org/info/report/r04.htm, which discusses overcrowding, privatization, physical brutality by guards, sexual abuse, poor healthcare, juvenile corrections, and the improper use of restraints and stun devices. For the risk of rape in prison, see *No Escape*.

[132] Article 80. The Standard Minimum Rules for the Treatment of Prisoner are nonbinding; they were adopted by the U.N. Economic and Social Council in 1957. In addition, the ICCPR mandates that "the reform and social re-adaptation of prisoners" be an "essential aim" of incarceration, ICCPR, Article 10.

[133] Article 62.

[134] *No Escape*, http://www.hrw.org/reports/2001/prison/report3.html#_1_16.

[135] See for example Louis Henkin, "U.S. Ratification of Human Rights Conventions: The Ghost of Senator Bricker," 89 *A.J.I.L.* (1995).

[136] See the United Nations Treaty Collection for a list of the United States' reservations and declarations to the ICCPR, available at http://www.unhchr.ch/html/menu3/b/treaty5_asp.htm.

ratification of the ICCPR and the Convention Against Torture... are among the longest and most detailed of any country that has ratified the two instruments." [137]

In terms of prisoners' rights, US reservations to CAT and ICCPR in essence declare that the treaties' prohibitions of torture and cruel, inhuman or degrading treatment or punishment apply only to the extent that the provisions cover acts already barred under the US Constitution as interpreted by the Supreme Court. Thus, with the CAT, the US ratification was subject to the reservation that it be held to the "cruel and unusual punishment" standard, which is far stricter than most interpretations of "cruel, inhuman or degrading treatment" as described in the torture convention. [138]

As a State party to the ICCPR and the CAT, US is obligated periodically to report on its compliance with the ICCPR and the CAT to the relevant treaty bodies, the United Nations Human Rights Committee [139] and the United Nations Committee Against Torture, [140] respectively. The US submitted its first ICCPR compliance report to the Human Rights Committee in 1994. [141] The US submitted its CAT compliance report in 1999, four years late; the second report was due in 2001 but has not been filed as of this writing. [142]

The compliance reports have not yielded much factual information on actual conditions and violations. [143] For example, the Human Rights Committee stated in its review of the US's compliance report that it regretted that " while containing comprehensive information on the laws and regulations ... at the federal level, the report contained few references to the implementation of Covenant rights at the state level." [144] In terms of pris-

---

[137] No Escape, http://www.hrw.org/reports/2001/prison/report3.html#_1_16.

[138] Henkin, 342. See also Geer, 95-100.

[139] States party to the ICCPR must report to the Human Rights Committee within one year of the entry into force of the ICCPR for the state, and then at the Committee's request, which is generally every five years.

[140] States party to the CAT must report to the Committee Against Torture within one year after the entry into force of the Convention for the State and thereafter supplementary reports every four years on any new measures taken and such other reports as the Committee may request (Article 19).

[141] According to the Office of the High Commissioner for Human Rights Treaty Body Database, the US's second ICCPR compliance report was due in 1998, but has not yet been submitted, see http://www.unhchr.ch/tbs/doc.nsf/.

[142] Office of the High Commissioner for Human Rights Treaty Body Database, available at: http://www.unhchr.ch/tbs/doc.nsf/

[143] No Escape, http://www.hrw.org/reports/2001/prison/report3.html#_1_16.

[144] Concluding Observations of the Human Rights Committee: United States of America, CCPR/C/79/Add.50; A/50/40, paras. 266-304 (1995).

ons and prisoners' rights, the Human Rights Committee expressed concern about overcrowding, sexual abuse of female prisoners and conditions of maximum security facilities. The Committee Against Torture expressed the same concerns about female prisoners and maximum security prisons, adding the use of electro-shock devices and restraint chairs on prisoners. The Committee also stated that it was concerned about

> ...the number of cases of police ill-treatment of civilians, and ill-treatment in prisons (including instances of inter-prisoner violence). Much of this ill-treatment by police and prison guards seems to be based upon discrimination.[145]

---

[145] Conclusions and Recommendations of the Committee against Torture: United States of America, A/55/44, paras.175-180 (2000).

X. CONCLUSION AND RECOMMENDATIONS

In their own words, here are what some respondents had to say on the subject of the justice of the Rockefeller drug laws:

PY, a 46-year-old man, served the longest consecutive sentence in the sample: 11 years of a 15 year-to-life sentence before his sentence was commuted by Governor Pataki. Prior to his arrest, he was a habitual cocaine user and had no criminal record. PY was convicted at trial for a Class A1 drug felony for a sale of just over two ounces of cocaine to an undercover police officer. He was incarcerated in maximum security prisons. On drug addicts sent to prison under the Rockefeller drug laws, PY said, *"treating addiction with incarceration is tantamount to treating dandruff with decapitation."* He added, *"with an addicted population, don't incarcerate them, teach them how to live.... It is more criminal to destroy all the positive things of an addict's life by incarcerating a person."*

OP, a 38-year-old recovering addict who cycled in and out for felony drug sale and possession charges, said, *"Don't let us go from prison to being set up again in society."* He added:

> *If you have the right sentence and the right programs for selling, they'd have better statistics.... Prison won't help my problem. It's abusive. Programs will help, prison won't. You need something to keep your mind occupied. Drug therapy. Better employment services.*

AD, a 54-year-old man, who had cycled in and out of prison his whole life, said he hoped this study would have an impact so that others wouldn't have to go *"through a prison system that's not geared to their development as a human being."* He was concerned that many people did not understand the damage done in prison: *"you become detached, isolationist, anti-human... where you know people are not important; your own life is not important."* This does not lead to behaviors that bring change, but *"you're only going to relapse into the same behaviors that sent you to prison, or you're going to die."*

In conclusion, there are a number of misconceptions held by proponents of the laws relating to drug crimes in New York. This research helps expose ten myths about mandatory sentences such as the Rockefeller drug laws.

Ten Myths about the Rockefeller Drug Laws

Myth 1: Incarceration Serves as a Deterrent. New York State punishes drug offenses severely, yet sees no parallel reduction in offending. No person interviewed for this research mentioned fear of prison as a factor in their decision to engage or desist in drug-related or other crimes. The most common reason people gave for initially selling drugs was economic: selling drugs offered a quicker and more secure path to economic independence than any legitimate employment. Respondents described growing up in environments where criminal activity was prevalent, even in those families that abhorred such behavior. As noted above, almost all the people in the sample had committed multiple offences and, while they spoke about hating being incarcerated, with little exception, that misery did not seem to serve a preventive effect once they were released from custody.

Myth 2: Harsh Punishments are Justified because of the Severity of the Drug Crimes. Not surprisingly, no one in the sample believed that the severity of the Rockefeller drug laws was appropriate for the offenses they committed. While drug addiction and the drug trade are serious problems for society as a whole as well as local communities, they are certainly no more serious than violent offences such as robbery, rape and assault. Yet New York mandates severe sentences for drug-related crimes, while maintaining some judicial discretion for violent offences. Everyone interviewed for this research was a drug user and nearly everyone faced long-term addiction, indicating a public health problem more than a criminal justice problem. Yet drug addiction – in low-income and predominantly nonwhite neighborhoods in New York – is treated first as a law and order problem and all too often the health implications of the drug trade are ignored or treated with inadequate resources.

Myth 3: Tough Drug Laws Reduce Drug-Related Crime. People interviewed for this report described their relatively minor roles in local drug economies and spoke about the ease of finding work selling or holding drugs. Most people sent to prison for one, three or even seven years and longer committed petty offenses, typically for sale or possession of only a few grams of illegal drugs. The subjects referred to the apparently never-ending source of low-level labor to perform their drug-related jobs after they were taken off the streets and sent to prison. In addition, the majority of subjects were spending their lives cycling in and out of prison. This research parallels findings from previous studies that show no significant correlation between high arrest and prosecution rates and reductions in offending.

Myth 4: Harsh Punishments Help People Stop Using Drugs. Respondents in the sample spoke about their lifelong efforts to overcome drug addiction. While prison was frequently the first place that many people in the sample received drug treatment, no one felt that prison conditions were ideal for rehabilitation or that being treated harshly and with disrespect as they were in prison was helpful to attain sobriety. Most people in this research had served multiple prison terms and had continued to struggle with addiction in spite of any treatment they received while incarcerated. Respondents overwhelmingly cited the importance of family support in regaining the self-respect and dignity they felt that they needed to stop using drugs. Notably, family support is particularly difficult to maintain during incarceration since prisons are typically located far from inmates' home communities and are difficult and costly for family members reach.

Myth 5: Drug Laws are Fairly Applied. This research confirmed findings from other research that indicates that the people who are arrested, prosecuted, convicted and incarcerated for drug crimes are increasingly likely to be non-white and poor. In particular African-Americans are seriously over-represented in the criminal justice system across the nation and in New York, where approximately three-quarters of the inmate population comes from a handful of New York City minority communities. Yet despite this racial gap in incarceration, the most reliable statistics on drug abuse in America indicate that there are few differences in drug use across the primary racial groups. Severe drug sentences are fueled by laws that promote intensive policing of poor, minority communities, while white, affluent drug users can maintain their drug habits using computers, telephones, pagers and delivery services that make any street-level activity (where arrest is much more likely) unnecessary.

Myth 6: If a Person Wants to Stop Using Drugs, They Can. In spite of a growing and useful research literature about drug addiction, many of the details of how addiction works and how it can be overcome remain unknown. Contrary to simplistic messages such as 'just say no,' respondents told researchers that the relief, pleasure, income and social connections of drugs continued to prove very difficult to resist in spite of their best efforts to stay sober. Most people in the research had long histories of drug use but were also keenly aware of the harm associated with their addictions. The abstract ideal of stopping drug use was not enough to simple cut drugs out of people's lives. Some respondents felt they were securely abstinent, but many others were more cautious, citing a one-day-at-a-time philosophy to recovery.

Myth 7: Prisoners Can Get Drug Treatment if They Want It. While some drug treatment is available in New York state prisons, it is not comprehensive, consistent or available enough to address the needs of New York's inmate population, more than sixty percent of whom are in need of treatment. New York City's primary jail has recently cut its principal drug treatment as a result of budgetary demands. Drug treatment that does exist varies in content and quality, but the state does not have either a rigorous screening system or a funded research agenda to understand the prison system's treatment capacity and needs. People interviewed for this research described being taken out of treatment when they were moved to different prisons, mediocre treatment, and a dearth of continuity in treatment – all of which are targeted as responsible for low success rates in the drug treatment literature.

Myth 8: Tough Drug Laws Help Poor Communities. Drug use exists in all communities, but poor communities are targeted for increased police activity and consequently members of these communities make up the majority of the prison population. Respondents described family relationships that were unstable because of parents' incarceration and further destabilized when the respondent was incarcerated. Many communities have lost significant percentages of their men, and a growing percentage of women, to incarceration. The cumulative impact of targeted policing coupled with severe sentencing was demonstrated in this research by the prevalence of social networks that extended between the New York City neighborhoods where research subjects live, to the jails and prisons in which they had been incarcerated.

Myth 9: New York State Prisons Maintain the Human Rights of Inmates. Respondents in this study report numerous cases of human rights abuses. People reported witnessing or themselves being the victim of: racial harassment including slurs, taunts, sexual groping; coerced sexual relationships including trading sex for goods; forced sexual intercourse; physical assault beyond what is necessary in a prison environment to maintain order; delayed and withheld medical and related care; and excessive use of isolation. Additionally, ex-prisoners continue to face punishments upon release from prison. Punishments such as exclusion of welfare and medical benefits and job discrimination are separate from court-ordered punishments and violate the right of a person to fair punishment as applicable at the time the offense is committed.

Myth 10: The Rockefeller Drug Laws are Just. For all of the reasons cited above, this research has demonstrated that mandatory and severe drug sentences are unfair to some of the citizens of New York and therefore unacceptable to all. Because of the intrinsic inequality with which these laws are applied, they sow the seeds of discontent and exacerbate racial and economic injustice and division among the people of New York. The laws are responsible for the continued stigmatization and marginalization of large portions of the state's minority populations and so undermine the wellbeing of New York and its communities.

Recommendations

To the United States Congress

- Increase funding for drug treatment alternatives to incarceration

- Eliminate post-incarceration punitive measures such as restrictions on public housing, federal education aid and other public assistance. These restrictions undermine the criminal justice policy by implying that punishment through the courts and prisons is not sufficient. They run counter to the goal of rehabilitation; in effect they assert that ex-prisoners don't deserve to be recipients of social benefits, regardless of the punishment they have undergone. And they destabilize communities by further depriving economically and socially disadvantaged areas of the resources necessary for individual members to maintain stable and socially productive lives.

To New York State

- New York should grant its judiciary the discretion to depart from statutory sentencing ranges for people convicted of nonviolent drug offenses who are not major players in drug sales operations. The laws should recognize differences in conduct, levels of danger to the community, and other factors relevant to sentencing.

- New York must increase the availability and use of alternatives for people convicted of drug offenses, especially nonviolent drug offenses like simple possession. These alternatives should include drug treatment and other rehabilitative services that adhere to, and seek to improve upon, best practices demonstrated in clinical literature. Prison should be the last rather than first alternative.

- Health professionals in the treatment field accept that people will relapse during the course of their recovery. However, the courts have typically regarded relapse as a failure of rehabilitative efforts and they have punished relapse by revoking the ATI sentence and imposing an incarceratory sentence, frequently even harsher than the original prison sentence. If a person relapses while in an alternative to incarceration program, and there has been no new arrest for crime committed, New York should ensure that there be repeated attempts to engage the person in treatment. In addition, people should never face a sentence any more severe than they would absent the ATI program for either a drug relapse or for committing a technical violation (rule infraction) while they are in an ATI program. Finally, treatment programs should specify their policies on drug use relapse to the courts, and programs should adhere to these policies.

- Substance abuse treatment should be appropriate to the assessed need of the individual and must be made available at levels that meet the demand for treatment, both inside and outside of prison. The state should increase funding for drug treatment both in and outside of prisons in order to develop more accurate assessment tools as well as to increase comprehensive drug treatment programs, expand existing treatment programs and assure high levels of efficacy through staff training. An investment in treatment, while perhaps costly in the short term, is less expensive than the likely cycle of incarceration that is highly predictable with an absence of treatment.

- Increase funding for poverty-reduction programs such as vocational training linked to job-placement and incentives to employers who hire ex-prisoners, especially in New York City where the majority of state prison inmates lived prior to and after incarceration. Vocational services should include career planning skills.

- Eliminate housing restrictions that penalize ex-prisoners and their families and prevent housing stability after release from prison.

- Develop and strengthen existing networks between the Department of Correctional Services and community-based employment services targeting ex-prisoners in order to link prison-based job training with post-release employment. Provide additional resources to support capacity growth for such agencies including the ability of these agencies to respond to the ongoing needs of ex-prisoners in the workplace.

- Assess the economic conditions and possibilities for upstate counties that have come to rely on prisons for jobs and related spending. Consider facilitating the development of alternative economies for upstate New York communities that have come to depend on prison construction and maintenance.

To the New York State Department of Correctional Services

- Ensure that prisoners receive the prevailing standard of drug treatment as in the community at large. Monitor and evaluate prison-based drug treatment for quality and eliminate ineffective programs.

- Develop uniform pre-release standards and protocols and monitor their implementation and outcome. Mandate release plans that include reliable housing, employment and drug treatment. Treatment has to be systematized, adhered to and monitored so that all staff are providing treatment according to a single program model based on research demonstrating what works.

- Ensure that prisoners receive the prevailing standard of quality in healthcare as in the community at large and that they receive a high continuity of healthcare when transferred between prisons.

- Establish policies and protocols to incarcerate people closer to home and develop family visitation programs to facilitate and increase family contact with inmates.

- Develop and implement sensitivity training for corrections staff based on best practices nation-wide and monitor it regularly. Such a system should make use of incentive-based behavior. Assess hate crime activity throughout prison system and develop trainings to educate Department of Correctional Services staff and emphasize the department's zero-tolerance policy towards racist and other hate-based behavior.

- Develop addiction assessment and linked system of continuum of treatment options. Corrections administrators typically put someone caught with drugs into solitary confinement and do not provide drug treatment. This is not effective in addressing underlying causes of drug use. Prison officials must address the availability of drugs and ongoing problem of addiction within prisons and eliminate policy that responds to drug use using solitary confinement (punishment) without therapy (treatment).

- Restore and expand funding for inmate education, job training and job development. Assess and coordinate these programs.

To New York State Division of Parole

- Eliminate the use of "return to custody" for parole violations related solely to drug use. This would be part and parcel of a general review of violation criteria to reduce officer discretion regarding punishment for violations and increase officer resources that can be used to stabilize a parolee at risk of return to criminal activity.

- Evaluate violation patterns with a sample of parole officers and use to develop training including incentive- and punishment-based supervision of parolees.

- Develop relationships with community-based organizations (CBOs); conduct outreach to expand the number of CBOs willing to work with ex-prisoners; and create and maintain computerized referral network.

- Increase parole contributions to advocacy for more inclusive services for ex-prisoners, including federal benefits, housing and employment.

- Conduct community outreach to support and inform communities receiving ex-prisoners. Regularly send representative to community-based meetings to answer community concerns and establish trust.

To the Office of Court Administration

- Develop guidelines for the use of incarceration and other sentences. Assess concerns and needs of judiciary in order to maximize judicial ability and willingness to consider the impact of sentence decision on the community. It would be important to know what kind of information judges need in order to exercise discretion (e.g., treatment, rehabilitation, impact on community, victim, broader social circles of offender). Develop materials, visits, and trainings to inform judges and attorneys about the conditions of incarceration and the rehabilitative content of jails, prisons and alternative programs. Develop and implement annual training of judiciary on sentencing and supervisory options.

- Assess and expand the role of drug courts and other alternative sentencing options to include drug offenders convicted of more serious crimes, including those who have prior violent felony convictions.

- Assess the impact of regular and intensive supervision on offenders sentenced to community-based sanctions.

To New York City, Office of the Criminal Justice Coordinator

- Support the operation and expansion of alternatives to incarceration through contracts, lobbying efforts and information campaigns.

- Commit to facilitating city agency coordination of prisoner reentry services.

- Explore the utility of responsible use of shared data-systems to increase service accessibility to ex-prisoners and their families.

- Support and promote service delivery to ex-prisoners among organizations (social service, job development, drug treatment) not currently working with this population.

- Support community outreach to neighborhoods with high arrest rates to assist in reentry from prison.

- Increase public awareness campaigns about the effects of Rockefeller drug law sentencing on New York City communities.

To New York City Department of Correction

- Restore, monitor, and evaluate jail-based drug treatment. Develop uniform pre-release standards and protocols and monitor their implementation and outcomes. Mandate release plans that include discussion of and referral to housing, employment and drug treatment assistance.

- Assess and monitor training for corrections staff to reduce rights abuses. Such a system should make use of incentive-based behavior.

- Address the availability of drugs and the ongoing problem of addiction within jails and expand efforts to combat drug use that focus on treating addiction as well as punishment.

To New York City Police Department

- Examine policing policies that target low-income African-American and Latino communities for drug enforcement and "quality of life" (arrests for minor offenses) efforts. Assess the racial implications of such policies through independent review by researchers and community-based agencies as well as Police Department staff.

- Expand efforts to build community relations in low-income and non-white communities in particular.

- Prioritize racial sensitivity training for all officers and include both negative and positive incentives in this effort. Cooperate with the New York City Civilian Complaint Review Board and external review of department practices in this effort.

To Direct Service Providers

- Develop assessment tools to improve utility of standard intake interview. Many of the people interviewed for this study discussed plans that were ambitious but also disconnected. Offenders returning from jail or prison, as well as those who receive lesser sentences need assistance in planning on how to take care of themselves. For some this means realistic skill development, for others benefits coordination and housing, for others it means mending family relationships. Typically intake tools gather a wealth of information that is not used except on a triage basis.

- Network with other service providers. New York has dozens of service agencies that work with ex-prisoners. Shared resources, a shared referral network and established data-sharing practices would maximize the number of clients served. Sharing resources would also allow agency specialization (e.g. in literacy training, in job development, in benefit coordination), which would increase the efficacy of services.

- Pursue funds and allocate staff time to assess and improve treatment philosophy and method. Drug addiction treatment, educational and vocation development and the development of a social ethic (i.e. to avoid criminal activity) are all in need of improvement. While much has been done in these areas, agencies remain on the front lines of innovation and need to take seriously the long-term goals of improving treatment models and disseminating those that are effective. The effort to improve treatment includes: conducting staff evaluation; supporting staff who are interested in furthering their education; attending national trainings and research conferences; conducting and evaluating internal trainings and retreats; and disseminating research and best-practices findings and literature.

- Increase community outreach and services targeting ex-prisoner reintegration into their neighborhoods.

APPENDIX I

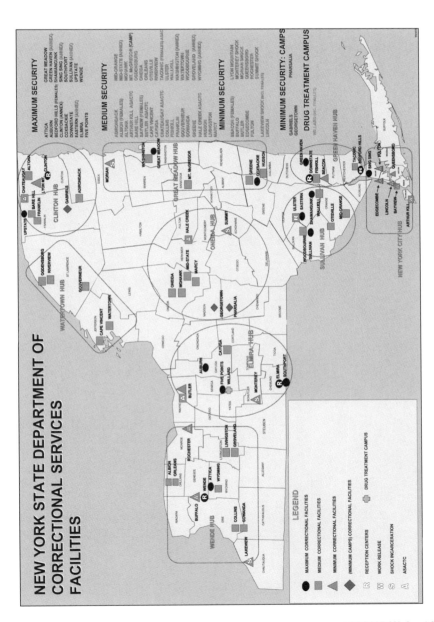

APPENDIX II

Physicians for Human Rights/The Fortune Society

The Effects of Mandatory Minimum Sentencing for Drug Offenses on Lives of Ex-Offenders

Physicians for Human Rights and The Fortune Society ask you to participate in this research study. The purpose is to better understand the effects of mandatory minimum drug-law sentencing on the lives of those convicted of these offenses and to educate the public and policymakers on this issue. To be eligible for the study, participants must have served at least a year in a New York state prison for a non-violent drug offense, with this the only or most recent felony conviction, be ex-offenders of a drug offense who served at least a year in a New York state prison and have no other conviction for a violent crime.

Your participation will remain confidential. All personal identifiers, including this consent form, will be kept in secure files. Your name and other identifying information will not be used in any public reports or materials.

Voluntary Participation, Withdrawal and Alternatives

Your participation in this study is completely voluntary and you are under no obligation to participate in the study. You have the right to withdraw from it at any time. If you are a client of Fortune and withdraw from the study, you will remain a client and not suffer any adverse effect on the services that you receive at Fortune or its network of providers.

Procedures

Participants will be asked for candid, detailed descriptions of their experiences before, during and after the time they served in prison. The study addresses family and community relationships, living situation, work status, income level, health, drug involvement and social activities before and after incarceration and experiences in prison as well. We estimate the interview will last about two hours. At the end of the interview, you will be asked whether you would like to participate in a subsequent interview that will be videotaped. If you agree, we will ask you to give us contact information so we can contact you for a second interview. You are free to refuse the request for the second interview and still participate in the first interview.

Confidentiality

The Fortune Society and Physicians for Human Rights are committed to protecting your privacy and the privacy of the information these organizations collect about you, and we have taken steps to minimize the risk of such unauthorized disclosure. These steps include training staff to keep your information private, securing paper records in secure files and putting into place measures that secure data on each agency's computer network and minimize the chance that an unauthorized user can gain access. If you say you are likely to harm yourself or someone else or give specific information on child abuse, Fortune and PHR are obligated to report the information to appropriate authorities.

Risks

If you have suffered painful and/or traumatic experiences, you may experience discomfort in telling us about them. If you want, we can seek the assistance of a counselor at Fortune. At any time you are free to pause, not answer a question or decline to continue the interview.

In addition, we cannot guarantee absolute confidentiality. However, PHR has conducted sensitive research on victims of human rights abuses for more than 15 years and scrupulously maintained the confidentiality of those who share information with us. Fortune has had more than 30 years of experience providing services to ex-offenders and maintaining the privacy of client information, as well as more than 10 years of experience conducting program evaluation that has included the collection of sensitive data. There is a risk of breach of confidentiality of the information you share with research staff. The Fortune Society and Physicians for Human Rights are committed to protecting your privacy and the confidentiality of the information it collects about you. Fortune and PHR have taken specific steps to minimize the risk of such unauthorized disclosure, as described above. In the past, PHR has successfully fought subpoenas by US authorities for access to research information. PHR and Fortune would fight any such effort by authorities for access to the research information, although we consider it highly unlikely any authorities would seek such access. As described above, we cannot guarantee absolute confidentiality,

Benefits, Financial Incentive

There are no specific individual benefits to participation in this study, except the $50 compensation (in the form of a gift certificate) for your time and travel expenses, which you will receive after completing the interview.

Questions

If you have further questions, comments or concerns about the study or the informed consent process, you may speak to Stanley Richards, Deputy Executive Senior Director, The Fortune Society, at 212/691-7554; or Dr. Vincent Iacopino, Research Director, Physicians for Human Rights at 702/547-1683

Consent

I voluntarily agree to participate in this study. I will be given a copy of this form after it is signed.

_____

Participant's signature   *Date*

_____

Participant's name (please print)

_____

Interviewer's signature and date

_____

Co-interviewer's signature and date

APPENDIX III

INTERVIEWS WITH EX-OFFENDERS
PHR-FORTUNE STUDY

My name is _____ and my colleague's is _____ . We work with The Fortune Society, an ex-offender service agency, and Physicians for Human Rights, a human rights organization based in Boston. We are studying the effects of New York's laws mandating sentences for people convicted of drug offenses. We are interviewing Fortune's clients to better understand how imprisonment for such offenses affects people's lives and to make the public and policy makers aware of these effects. We are interviewing recent Fortune clients who were released since 1996 after serving at least a year for a drug offense and were not convicted of a violent offense at the same time. We would like to interview you about your experiences. The interview will take about 2 hours of your time and you will receive a $50 gift certificate to Old Navy as a thank you for your participation upon completion of the interview. The information used from the interviews will be compiled in a report and other public materials. Some of the people we interview may be asked to consider returning for a second, videotaped interview. At the end of today's interview, you will be asked to provide your contact information for this purpose, but you do not have to share any information that you do not wish to. If you agree to today's interview, you are not obligated to participate in the second, videotaped interview. We will ask at the close of the interview if you would be willing to give us contact information; because we will call some of the people who provide contact information and ask if they would be willing to be videotaped in order to produce a video report.

However, you do not need to provide your contact information to participate in today's interview. Your participation will remain completely confidential and we will not use your name or other identifying information in any way unless you authorize us to do so. Fortune and PHR have taken security measures to protect the researcher's paper and computer files. Consent forms and any contact information will be kept in separate secure files.We will ask at the close of the interview if you want to be identified and will give us contact information.

If you have suffered painful and/or emotional events, in telling us about them you may experience discomfort. At any time, you are free to pause, not answer a question or terminate the interview. We can seek a counselor here at Fortune if you feel you need one. Your participation will have no impact on services you are receiving or might receive from Fortune in the future. You are free to decline to participate, but we hope you will participate in the study. Do you have any questions before we begin? Do we have your permission to begin? If so, I would like to kindly request that you read this consent form and sign it.

0   Consent provided (circle ONE): No _____0

                                                      Yes _____1

1   Location Code   _____(1, 2, 3...)

2A   Interviewer ID   _____(1, 2, 3...)

2B   Co-interviewer ID   _____(1,2,3...)

3   Respondent code   _____(1-200)

4   Date   _____(day)_____(month), 2003

5   Participation Outcome: (Circle ONE)

        Eligible/Survey Complete = 1

        Not Eligible   = 2

        Not Available/No Show = 3

        Refusal   = 4a=Lack Time;
                                        4b=Fear Reprisal;
                                        4c=Opposed to Study;
                                        4d=Other_____

        Unable to Complete   = 5a=Interrupted; 5b=Emotional;
                                        5c=Safety; 5d=Other_____6

6. Gender   Female 1

                      Male 2

We want to hear from you about the differences and similarities between your life before prison and after – for example your work and relationships with family members – and your experiences in prison. But before we get to that discussion, we will begin with some specific questions.

7. What is your current age?   _____ years

8. What is your current marital status? (Circle ONE)

Single..............................1
Married.........................2
Divorced......................3
Widowed.......................4
Separated.....................5
Other:..........................6

9. What is your race or ethnicity?

African American.........1
Hispanic/Latino............2
Asian.............................3
Caucasian.....................4
Other (specify)..............5

10A. How many years of school have you completed?_____
(GED = 12, any college = 13, Associates degree = 14, Bachelors degree = 16. If they have more than a few courses in college, but no degree, have them estimate the number of years and add to 12)

10B. Check here if earned a GED _____ (make a check mark)

11. Besides your recent drug sentence, have you served state or federal prison time for any other offenses?

No _____0
Yes _____1

12. Please indicate your employment* status currently and before** ever going to prison, and [IF APPLICABLE] before the (latest) drug sentence. Also please estimate your average monthly income from the employment and then your average monthly overall income from employment and other sources for each time period. _____

[* EMPLOYMENT is regular work for pay that may be "under the table", but not criminal as in drug sales, selling stolen merchandise or other similar activities.

** BEFORE – means the average for the 6 months before ever going to prison or for the 6 months before the (latest) drug conviction.]

	Employed or unemployed?	Monthly Income from employ. $/month	Add'l Income $/month	Source
Work Before Prison				
IF APPLICABLE Work Before (latest) drug sentence				
Current Work				

Unemployed = 1
Employed = 2 (Specify)

Govt benefits = 1
Illegal activities = 2
Other = 3 (Specify)

13A. *How many children do you have?* (including biological and adopted)

13B. *Please indicate the number of dependents you supported before ever going to prison, after prison, and [IF APPLICABLE] just before your(latest) drug sentence, as well as the number of children you supported at each time. Also please indicate the number of people you lived with before and after prison, and [IF APPLICABLE] just before your(latest) drug sentence, as well as the number of children you lived with at each time.*

IF APPLICABLE

# Dependents/# Children You Supported Before any Prison time	# Dependents/ # Children You Supported before the (latest) drug sentence	# Dependents/ # Children You Supported After Prison
/	/	/

IF APPLICABLE

# Dependents/# Children You Lived With Before any Prison time	# Dependents/ # Children You Lived With before the (latest) drug sentence	# Dependents/ # Children You Lived With After Prison
/	/	/

14. *Please indicate whether you were a regular participant (at least twice a month) in a community group, (i.e. religious group, school, sports team, parents group, neighborhood association, or other) before and after prison and [IF NEEDED] before your (latest) drug sentence. Also please provide the names of the group(s)*

IF APPLICABLE

Community Groups	Participation Before Prison	Participation Before (latest) drug sentence	Participation After Prison
13a. Religious group			
13b. School			
13c. Sports team			
13d. Neighborhood association			
13e. Other (specify)			
13f. Other (specify)			

No = 0, Yes = 1

15. *Please indicate whether you ever registered and voted before and after prison.*

Did you ever register to vote before ever going to prison?	Did you ever vote before ever going to prison?	Did you ever register to vote after prison?	Did you ever vote after prison?

No = 0, Yes = 1

16. *Did you know felons must go through a special process to register to vote?* _____ (No = 0, Yes = 1)

17. *Please indicate any prior the non-violent drug felony offenses that you have been convicted of and led to sentences in a state or federal prison.*

Offense Convicted for	Time Served	State	Place Released from	Date Released
16a.				
16b.				
16c.				
16d.				
16e.				
16f.				
16g.				
16h.				
16i.				

A I felony possession/sale..........1
A II felony possession/sale..........2
B felony possession/intent
to sell/sale. 3
C felony possession/sale..........4
D felony possession/sale..........5
Other (write out other offenses
such as assault, burglary,
fraud etc)(specify) 6

\# Yrs/Mos.
conviction)

(write 'fed',
for a federal

18. *Was the most recent conviction from*
a plea bargain 1
a guilty verdict at trial........2
other (specify) 3

19. *What is your current parole status?* (Circle ONE):
Not released with any supervision......................1
Completed supervision (was on parole)..............2
Currently under supervision..............................3
Other (specify): _____.................4

20. *How did you end up at Fortune?* (Circle ALL that apply)
Mandated/required by Parole terms or officer 1
Suggested by parole officer or other state official.........................2
Self referral, or learned about Fortune from a friend or inmate 3
Other (specify): _____ 4

Semi-Structured Questions

At this time, we would like to ask you some questions about your life experiences before, during and after imprisonment. We will ask questions about relationships with family, friends and community, about work and school, work, income, your living situation and health, involvement with drugs and future plans. In answering these questions, please provide as much detail as you can to help us understand how prison may have affected your life.

Let's begin with life before you were imprisoned [for the most recent drug offense, if participant has been to prison or jail other times] *and proceed in chronological order as much as possible.*

A. Life Before Prison

We would like to hear what life was like for you before you ever served time in prison. Would you tell us about your:

- Living Situation (home/shelter, financial capabilities/problems)
- Relationships with family – especially any children you have, friends, and the community
- Work experiences (formal and informal)
- Education (past and present experiences and future interests)
- Social Activities (sports, hobbies, interests, religious practices, voting, etc.)
- Drug involvement
- Health, physical and mental
- Future Plans

B. Life in Prison

Tell us about life in prison. What was it like for you? [Be sure to distinguish the most recent prison experience from other significant past prison experiences.]

- Did you participate in any education, work or training programs and did they have an impact on you?
- Did it serve a useful purpose? For you? For society?
- Were you able to maintain relationships, for example with any children you have or other family, or make new relationships there?
- How did your health (physical and mental) and health care change?
- Were you involved or were others involved in drugs in prison
- Did your experiences in prison change you? If so, how?

- How did your time in prison affect you emotionally? Has this changed since then? If so how?
- Did you experience or witness any abuse? Please explain.
- Can you tell us any particular positive or negative experiences?

C. Life Since Prison

How has your life changed since serving time in prison? Let's talk first about changes you may experienced after your first imprisonment and then discuss possible changes after any other time you may have served, specifically what your life was like before serving your (latest) drug sentence.[Be sure to track changes over time for each of the following questions.]

- Living Situation (home/shelter, financial capabilities/problems)
- Relationships (family – especially children, friends, community engagement)
- Work experiences (formal and informal)
- Education (past and present experiences and future interests
- Social Activities (sports, hobbies, interests, religious practices, voting, etc.)
- Drug involvement
- Future Plans
- Has your health (physical and mental) changed since you were in prison or since before prison? If so, how?

D. For participants with a history of time served for additional offenses ONLY:

- *Of the prison terms that you have served, which one, or ones, had the most effect on your life? Please explain.* [Consider whether early incarceration had more of an effect than later incarceration versus additive effects for each period of incarceration.]

E. For participants with a history of time served for prior violent offenses ONLY:

- *Do you think that time you served for a prior violent offense had more of an impact on your life than the time you just served for the drug offense? Please explain.*

F. *There are people who claim that the best way to deal with the drug problem in the US is to be tough on crime – That is, to give long sentences for even non-violent drug offenders who are not major traffickers. What do you have to say about that?*

G. *There are people who say that reform of drug sentencing should be considered only for non-violent drug offenders. What do you have to say about that?*

H. *Do you have anything else that you would like to add?*

(Interviewers: Make payment to participant at this point)

INTEREST IN SECOND INTERVIEW

In the next few months, we plan to start videotaping some of the interviews of people who have participated in this study. The questions will be very similar to the ones I asked you today, but the interview will be recorded on videotape. If participants would like their faces and/or voices concealed, that would be possible. Can we contact you about the possibility of interviewing you on videotape?

Consent to contact for video interview provided (circle ONE):

    No _____0

    Yes _____1

If yes, obtain contact information:

    Name: _____

    Tel: _____

    Address: _____

    Email: _____

RESEARCHERS: Keep this information apart from the questionnaire and the other research data.